Renal Diet Cookbook for Beginners:

Help Your Kidneys Unwind with Low Phosphorus, Potassium, and Sodium Recipes | Spyhnx Method

TABLE OF CONTENTS

1 INTRODUCTION

1.1 What are the kidneys and their function?

The kidney is an integral component of the human body. Significant illness or even death could result from a malfunctioning kidney. The function and structure of each kidney are extremely complex. They carry out two essential functions: removing poisonous and harmful wastes and maintaining the equilibrium of potassium, sodium, chemicals, minerals, fluids, and other substances.

Organ System of the Kidney

By eliminating harmful waste and extra water from the body, the kidneys create urine. Each kidney produces urine, which travels via the ureter and being removed by the urethra first, then the bladder. Both men and women typically have two kidneys.

- The kidneys are situated on either side of the spine, on the upper and lower sides of the abdomen (see diagram). The lower ribs shield them from injury.
- The kidneys are two bean-shaped organs that are typically located deep within the belly, where they are not palpable. The kidney of an adult measures roughly 10 cm long, 6 cm wide, and 4 cm thick. 150–170 grams is the usual weight of a kidney.
- The ureters are the tubes that carry urine from the kidneys to the bladder. Each ureter is a hollow tube-like structure that is roughly 25 cm long and is made up of certain muscles.
- The lower and anterior region of the abdomen contains the urine bladder, a hollow muscle-filled structure. It serves as a urine storage tank.
- About 400–500 ml of pee can be stored in an adult urinary bladder before the need to pass urine sets in.
- During the act of urinating, the pee in the bladder is expelled through the urethra. The urethra is considerably longer in males than it is in females.
- Every day, we eat a variety of foods in various amounts.
- Every day, our bodies' water, salt, and acid contents change.
- Food is continuously transformed into energy, which results in the production of hazardous poisonous chemicals.
- These elements cause alterations in the body's fluid, electrolyte, and acid composition.

What are the kidney's functions?

Urine production and blood purification are the kidney's two primary functions. Waste materials and other substances that the body does not need are excreted by each kidney. The following list includes a description of the kidney's main roles.

Elimination of waste materials

The primary function of the kidney is to remove waste from the blood, cleaning it.

We eat foods high in protein. The body needs protein to develop and heal. Protein, however, causes the body to generate waste. These waste products build up in the body and are retained there, much to the way the body retains poison. Each kidney filters blood and dangerous waste before excreting it in urine. Two significant waste products that are simple to quantify in the blood are creatinine and urea. Their "values" in blood tests reveal how well the kidneys are working. Blood tests will show elevated levels of urea and creatinine when both kidneys are failing.

removing extra fluid

The body's ability to hold onto the water it needs to survive while eliminating extra water as urine is the kidney's secondary function.

When the kidneys fail, they are unable to eliminate this extra water. Swelling is caused by the body having too much water.

The management of several minerals and substances, such as bicarbonate, calcium, phosphorus, magnesium, sodium, potassium, hydrogen, and calcium as well as the maintenance of a typical physiological fluid composition, are two other crucial functions of the kidneys.

While changes in potassium levels can have a substantial negative impact on the heart's rhythm and how well the muscles perform, variations in sodium levels can have an impact on a person's mental state. For healthy bones and teeth, optimum calcium and phosphorus levels must be maintained.

regulating blood pressure

By controlling the body's salt and water balance, the hormones renin, angiotensin, aldosterone, prostaglandin, and others that the kidneys generate play crucial roles in maintaining stable blood pressure management. In a patient with renal failure, issues with hormone production and the regulation of salt and water might result in high blood pressure.

synthesis of red blood cells

Red blood cell development requires erythropoietin, another hormone generated in the kidneys (RBC). Poor erythropoietin production results from renal failure, which also results in low RBC production, which results in low haemoglobin levels (anaemia).This is the reason why individuals with renal failure do not experience an increase in haemoglobin levels while taking iron and vitamin supplements.

to preserve strong bones

To develop and maintain strong, healthy bones as well as to absorb calcium from food, the body requires vitamin D. Vitamin D is transformed into its active form by the kidneys.Reduced amounts of active vitamin D due to kidney failure impede bone development and make bones more brittle. Growth delay in children could indicate renal disease.

1.2 What are Phosphorus, Potassium and sodium

Phosphorus

The mineral phosphorus, which is also available as a supplement, is naturally present in many foods. It serves the body in a multitude of capacities. It is essential for teeth, bone, and cell membranes. It maintains a healthy blood pH range and aids in enzyme activation. The mineral phosphorus is a component of DNA, RNA, and ATP, the body's main energy source. Additionally, it controls appropriate nerve and muscle activity, particularly in the heart. It functions as a structural component of our DNA as well.

The kidneys, bones, and intestines all play an important role in controlling the body's phosphorus levels. If the diet is low in phosphorus or too little is absorbed, the digestive tract becomes more efficient at absorbing phosphorus, the kidneys produce less phosphorus in urine, and the bones release their stores of phosphorus into the blood in an effort to maintain normal levels. These organs function the other way if the body has enough phosphorus reserves.

The Dietary Guidelines Allowance for adult males and females aged Nineteen or older is 700 mg per day. During breastfeeding and pregnancy, phosphorus needs per day are 700 mg.

Potassium

Potassium, a mineral element, is necessary for all physiological tissues. It is sometimes referred to as an electrolyte because it carries a minute electric charges that stimulates a range of cellular and neuronal processes. Many foods naturally contain potassium, and it can also be found in nutritional supplements. Its main function in the body is to maintain the fluid balance in our cells. On the other hand, sodium keeps the right fluid balance in cells. In addition, potassium encourages muscle contraction and aids in the maintenance of healthy blood pressure.

The AI is 2,300 mg for women between the ages of 14 and 18, and 2,600 mg for those over 19. Depending on their age, women who are pregnant or nursing have an AI between 2,500 and 2,900. Males aged 14 to 18 should take 3,000 mg of the AI, while men aged 19 and over should take 3,400 mg.

Sodium

Sodium chloride, also known as salt, is a compound made up of 60 percent chloride and 40 percent sodium. It adds flavour to food while stabilising and binding it. Due to the fact that bacteria cannot survive in salty environments, salt is also used as a food preservative. The human body requires a negligible amount of sodium to transmit nerve impulses, contract and relax muscles, and maintain the proper ratio of water and minerals. It is estimated that these essential processes require 500 mg of sodium per day from us. However, excessive salt consumption can lead to stroke, heart disease, and hypertension. Additionally, it may result in calcium losses, some of which may originate in the bones. Most Americans consume substantially more sodium than their bodies truly need, around 3400 mg (or 1.5 teaspoons) each day.

1.3 What are Renal diseases?

Chronic kidney disease: Chronic renal disease is the most prevalent type of kidney disease. The long-term status of chronic renal disease does not get better with time. It frequently results from excessive blood pressure.

renal stones: Kidney stones are another typical problem with the kidneys. They appear when minerals and other substances found in blood solidify to form solid masses in the kidneys (stones). Kidney stones often pass from the body through urination. Even though passing kidney stones can be painfully painful, major problems are rarely the result..

Glomerulonephritis: The glomeruli become inflamed in glomerulonephritis. Glomeruli are incredibly tiny kidney structures that filter blood. Glomerulonephritis can be brought on by illnesses, medications, or conditions that develop during or soon after birth (congenital abnormalities). Often, things get better on their own.

Renal polycystic disease: A genetic condition known as polycystic kidney disease results in an abundance of cysts—small fluid-filled sacs—growing inside the kidneys. Renal failure may result from these cysts' interference with kidney function.

Individual kidney cysts are fairly common and nearly often benign, it's crucial to remember that. Kidney disease with polycystic kidneys is a distinct, dangerous condition.

Infections of the urinary tract

Urinary tract infections are bacterial infections that can affect any component of the urinary system (UTIs). Urinary tract and bladder infections are the most common. They are easy to treat and hardly ever result in extra health problems. However, if these infections are left untreated, they may spread to the kidneys and cause renal failure.

1.4   What are the 5 Phase of the Chronic Kidney Disease (CKD)?

The level of renal function determines which of the 5 levels of chronic kidney disease (CKD) is present. Your estimated glomerular filtration rate (eGFR), a measurement of how well your kidneys are removing waste from your blood, can be used to establish the stage of CKD you are in. In order to delay the advancement of CKD and lengthen the time that your kidneys can continue to function, it is essential to take the best possible care of your health at each stage of the disease.

A KIDNEY DISEASE'S 5 STAGES

STAGE	eGFR	SYNTOMPS
1 CKD	≥90	little renal impairment
2 CKD	60<eGFR<89	mild decrease of renal function
3a and 3b	30<eGFR<59	mild to severe loss of renal function
4 CKD	15<eGFR<29	significant renal function decline
5 CKD	eGFR<15	Kidney failure or near-failure

Stage 1
The kidney damage is minimal in Stage 1 CKD. Despite any physical or visible damage to your kidneys, your kidneys are still functioning normally.
If you have stage 1 CKD and your estimated glomerular filtration rate (eGFR) is 90 or greater, your urine contains protein (i.e., your pee). If just protein is discovered in your system, you have Stage 1 CKD.
Stage 2
Your eGFR has decreased to a range of 60 to 89 in stage 2 CKD. You may not notice any changes in your health since your kidneys continue to filter your blood as they should. Even while it might not be possible to reverse the harm already done, there are some actions you can take to prevent more kidney injury. Your urine might or might not contain protein.
Stage 3
If you have kidney impairment that is mild to moderate and an eGFR between 30 and 59, you are considered to have stage 3 CKD. Your kidneys are not as effective as they should in removing waste and extra fluid from your circulation. As a result of the waste buildup, your body might develop a variety of health issues ranging from high blood pressure to bone damage. You might start to feel weak and weary, and your hands or feet might swell. Stage 3 CKD is separated into two substages based on eGFR: stage 3a (45-59) and stage 3b (60-69). (30 and 44). Many Stage 3 individuals who receive therapy and adopt healthy lifestyle changes do not advance to Stages 4 or 5.

Stage 4

If your estimated glomerular filtration rate (eGFR) is between 15 and 29, you are in stage 4 chronic renal disease. It's because your kidneys aren't filtering blood as well as they might. Buildup of these toxins can lead to hypertension, cardiovascular disease, and other conditions including osteoporosis and diabetes. A variety of symptoms, including lower back pain, edema in the hands and feet, and others, are likely to manifest. This is the last step before renal failure. Regular visits to a nephrologist are essential to stop kidney damage and get ready for prospective therapy for renal failure (kidney specialist).

Stage 5

Your kidneys are badly damaged in stage 5 CKD, and they are no longer capable of filtering waste from your blood. Your blood may become clogged with wastes, which can lead to a number of health issues, including:

- Elevated blood pressure
- Anemia (not really sufficient red blood cells in your body) ((Your body doesn't have enough red blood cells)
- Bone illness
- Heart condition
- elevated potassium
- a lot of phosphorus
- Acidosis metabolism (a buildup of acid in your body)

1.5 Why is necessary to treat this problem with the diet?

A renal-friendly diet can help you manage kidney illness and prevent kidney damage. Because your kidneys are less efficient at clearing waste from your body, it is vital that it prevents some minerals from accumulating in your body. A diet that is friendly to your kidneys can help you avoid other significant health issues, manage diabetes and excessive blood pressure, and stop kidney disease from worsening. Additionally, it guarantees that you receive the ideal ratio of nutrients to support you:

- Feel energised to complete your everyday tasks
- Avoid infection
- develop muscle
- Maintain a healthy weight.

1.6 What are the characteristics of the diet?

In order to reduce waste in the blood, those with impaired kidney function must follow a renal or kidney diet. Food and drink metabolites are absorbed into the bloodstream. Kidneys that aren't working properly can't filter blood or eliminate waste. The electrolyte balance of the patient might deteriorate if waste products are allowed to accumulate in the blood. Maintaining normal kidney function and delaying the onset of renal failure are both possible with a kidney-friendly diet.

Renal dieting means cutting back on salt, phosphorus, and protein. Consuming sufficient quantities of high-quality protein and limiting fluid consumption on a regular basis are other essential tenets of a renal diet. Some people may benefit from limiting their intake of potassium and calcium. Because every individual's physiology is unique, every patient must work with a renal dietician to develop a diet that is tailored to his or her specific needs.

1.7 Why Phosphorus, Potassium and sodium are dangerous for kidneys?

Extra phosphorus in your blood can be removed by healthy renal function. Having CKD makes it difficult for your kidneys to effectively remove phosphorus from your body. Your body can suffer harm from having too much phosphorous. Your body is altered by too much phosphorus in such a way that calcium is removed from your bones, weakening them.
Why should potassium and sodium intake be limited in kidney disease?
Consuming more sodium raises the intravascular blood volume, blood pressure, and ultimately the pressure in the glomeruli. Renal function is reduced as a result of the overall effect. Potassium operates in opposition to sodium, increasing sodium excretion as a result.

1.8 What are the exercise helpful for kidneys?

Walking: Almost everyone can benefit from this fairly safe kind of exercise. Anywhere and at any time are suitable for it. Start with a quick, simple five-minute walk that is very slow and quiet for those who never exercise. If there are no negative consequences, keep doing it for a week. After that, extend it for 10 minutes. Keep an eye on the body for any indications of stress or discomfort. If everything is fine, gradually extend the walk's duration.

Yoga and flexibility drills: Breathing drills can be done daily, and asanas assist the body stretching. Yoga and meditation both support maintaining a stress-free mind. Dialysis patients can readily perform sit-ups, squats, calf rises, dips, pull-ups, and other exercises.

Freestyle dancing: Play your favorite tunes and move to them, or watch videos online to learn some simple dance steps.

swimming Swimming is a fantastic type of exercise that is beneficial to everyone. The pressure on the joints is lessened in the water, making this a great approach to exercise the body without putting the joints through additional strain, which is possible when walking.

2 FOOD LIST: PERMITTED FOOD, FOOD TO AVOID AND LIMIT

Permitted food

- Bulgur
- Olive oil
- Buckwheat
- Garlic
- Egg whites
- Red grapes
- Sea bass
- Blueberries
- Cauliflower
- Shiitake mushrooms
- Pineapple
- Cranberries
- Turnips
- Radish
- Macadamia nuts
- Arugula
- Onions
- Bell peppers
- Skinless chicken
- Cabbage

Food to avoid

- Dark-colored soda
- Pretzels, chips, and crackers
- Avocados
- Dates, raisins, and prunes
- Packaged, instant, and premade meals
- Apricots
- Dairy
- Canned foods
- Potatoes and sweet potatoes
- Pickles, olives, and relish
- Tomatoes
- Oranges and orange juice
- Whole wheat bread
- Bananas
- Processed meats
- Swiss chard, spinach, and beet greens
- Brown rice

3 FAQ

What foods are prohibited from a renal diet?

Ham, bacon, sausage, hot dogs, lunch meats, chicken tenders, and ordinary canned soup should not be consumed. Read the product label to make sure the soups you consume don't include potassium chloride and are low in salt. Instead of eating the entire can, consume 1 cup.

Can you eat pasta on a renal diet?

Small portions of meat, chicken, or fish can be served as a side dish together with vegetables, grains, and pasta as the main course. In order to keep your protein intake in check, you can also include low-protein pastas.

On a renal diet, is rice permissible?

Rice is a fantastic option for the kidney diet because it gives out energy and has few minerals that are harmful for those who have kidney disease or are receiving dialysis.

On a renal diet, is milk okay to drink?

However, dairy products must be restricted in the diet of persons with chronic kidney disease (CKD). Low-fat milk, for example, has high quantities of calcium, potassium, and phosphorus that are bad for someone on a kidney diet.

Chronic renal disease can exist in people who exhibit no symptoms. False or True?

True. For a very long time, kidney disease may exist without exhibiting any symptoms. Over many years or even decades, kidney disease may gradually worsen. High blood pressure that is not under control and uncontrolled diabetes are the two most common causes of kidney damage.

Who is the name of the physician who focuses on kidney conditions?

A medical professional who focuses on kidney disorders is known as a nephrologist.

These experts can assist patients select the best therapy if renal failure does arise and may help patients avoid renal failure for years.

How many phases are there in kidney disease?

There are five stages to chronic renal illness.

Stage 1: Normal kidney function, however there are signs of renal disease.

- Stage 2: Mildly impaired kidney function and signs of renal disease are present.

Stage 3: Moderate renal function decline;

Stage 4: Significantly diminished renal function;

Stage 5: End-stage renal failure and significantly decreased kidney function

4 SHOPPING LIST FOR A WEEK OF DIET

- Bulgur
- Olive oil
- Buckwheat
- Garlic
- Egg whites
- Red grapes
- Sea bass
- Blueberries
- Cauliflower
- Shiitake mushrooms
- Pineapple
- Cranberries
- Turnips

5 BREAKFAST RECIPES

5.1 Deviled eggs

Preparation: 10 minutes
Cooking time: 00 minutes
Servings : 6

Ingredients

- light mayonnaise -3 tbsp. (45 g)
- Garlic -2 cloves
- ground cayenne pepper -2 tsp.(8g)
- parsley -1 tsp. (4g)
- Eggs, boiled – 6
- lime juice -1 1/2 tsp. (6 g)

Preparation

1. To extract the yolks from the eggs, cut them lengthwise. Half of the remaining yolks should be put in a bowl, and the other half should be thrown away.
2. Before adding the remaining parsley as a garnish, combine the mixture with egg whites.

Nutrition Information [per serving]

Calories 98| Fat 6.9 g|Total Carbohydrate 3.7g | Sugars 1.1g |Protein 5.8g| Potassium 90mg| Sodium 115 mg

Storage Place the airtight container and keep it in the refrigerator for up to five days.

Reheat: just defrost at room temperature for a few hours

5.2 Dilly Scrambled Eggs

Preparation: 05 minutes
Cooking time: 05 minutes
Servings : 1

Ingredients

- dill weed dried -1 tsp. (4 g)
- goat cheese - 1 tbsp.(15 g)
- Eggs -2
- black pepper -1/8 tsp.(1/2 g)

Preparation

1. Before adding the eggs to a non-stick skillet over medium heat, they should be beaten in a bowl first.
2. Dill weed and black pepper are added to the eggs.
3. Scramble the eggs after cooking them.
4. Before serving, sprinkle goat cheese crumbles on top.

Nutrition Information[per serving]

Calories 214| Fat 15.3g| Total Carbohydrate 1.4g| Sugars 1.1g |Protein17.3g|Potassium 178mg| Sodium 194 mg

Storage Put into airtight container and keep in refrigerator for up to five days.

Reheat: just defrost at room temperature for a few hours

5.3 Easy Apple Oatmeal

Preparation: 10 minutes
Cooking time: 00 minutes
Servings : 1

Ingredients

- quick-cooking oatmeal -1/3 cup (9 g)
- egg -1 large
- cinnamon -1/4 teaspoon (1 g)
- almond milk -1/2 cup (120 ml)
- Apple -1/2 medium

Preparation

1. Apple half, core, and finely cut.
2. In a big mug, mix oats, egg, and almond milk. With a fork, stir thoroughly. Add apple and cinnamon. Once more stir till combined.
3. Microwave on high for 2 minutes. Fluff with a fork. Cook for a further 30 to 60 seconds if necessary.
4. If you want your cereal to be thinner, stir in a little extra milk or water.

Nutrition Information

Calories   441

Fat 34.4g

Total Carbohydrate 29g

Total Sugars 16.1g

Protein 10.5g

Potassium 537 mg

Sodium 90 mg

Storage Put into airtight container and keep in refrigerator for up to five days.

Reheat: just defrost at room temperature for a few hours

5.4 Egg White French Toast

Preparation: 05 minutes

Cooking time: 05 minutes

Servings : 1

Ingredients

- Unsalted butter -1 tsp.(4 g)
- White bread – 1 slice
- Egg whites -1/2 cup (120 g)
- Maple syrup- 2 tbsp. (30 g)

Preparation

1. Over bread or an English muffin, spread butter. Divide into cubes.
2. Put buttered bread cubes in a bowl that may be used in the microwave.
3. Cover the bread with egg whites by doing so.
4. On top, drizzle some syrup.
5. Push up the edges of the egg white after one minute in the microwave to let the uncooked egg spill out.
6. Once the egg has set, microwave it for one more minute.

Nutrition Information[per serving]

Calories 136│Fat 4.3g│ Total Carbohydrate 9.4g│ Sugars 1.3g

│Protein14g│Potassium 208mg│Sodium 241 mg

Storage Put into airtight container and keep in refrigerator for up to five days.

Reheat: just defrost at room temperature for a few hours

5.5 Loaded Veggie Eggs

Preparation: 10 minutes

Cooking time: 05 minutes

Servings : 2

Ingredients

- fresh parsley and spring onion for garnish
- black pepper -1/4 tsp. (1 g)
- cauliflower -1 cup (100g)
- bell pepper -1/4 cup (38 g)
- whole eggs- 4
- Garlic clove -1
- Avocado oil -1 tbsp.(15 g)
- fresh kale - 3 cups (90 g)
- onion - 1/4 cup (40 g)

Preparation

1. Whip the eggs and pepper to a foamy, light consistency.
2. In a big skillet over medium heat, warm the oil.
3. Cook the peppers in the same skillet as the onions until they are soft and golden.
4. Add the kale, cauliflower, and garlic right away.
5. Reduce the heat to medium-low once the veggies have been sautéed, cover the skillet, and wait five minutes.
6. Combine the vegetables and add the eggs.
7. After the eggs have finished cooking, garnish with fresh parsley or spring onions.

Nutrition Information[per serving]

Calories 161│Fat 9g│Total Carbohydra te 7.4g   │Sugars 3.1g│Protein 13.8g│Potassium 585mg│ Sodium 175 mg

Storage Put into airtight container and keep in refrigerator for up to five days.

Reheat: just defrost at room temperature for a few hours

5.6 Blueberry Muffins

Preparation: 10 minutes
Cooking time: 30 minutes
Servings : 12

Ingredients

- unsalted butter -½ cup (113 g)
- fresh blueberries -2 ½ cups (362 g)
- Coconut milk - 2 cups (480 ml)
- salt -½ tsp. (2 g)
- coconut sugar -1 ¼ cups (225 g)
- almond flour -2 cups (84 g)
- Eggs -2
- baking powder -2 tsp. (8 g)

Preparation

1. Combine butter and sugar in a mixer on low speed until frothy and creamy.
2. After each addition, combine the eggs one at a time.
3. Gradually pour the milk into the dry ingredients after sifting them.
4. Add blueberries after hand crushing 1/2 cup of them. The last step is to carefully add the remaining blueberries.
5. Rub the muffin tins and the pan's surface with some vegetable oil. Place the muffin tins inside the pan.
6. Pour batter into each muffin cup to the top. the tops of the muffins with sugar.
7. Bake for 25 to 30 minutes at 375 °F (176 °C). Food should be allowed to cool in the pan for at least 30 minutes before being carefully removed.

Nutrition Information[per serving]
Calories 300|Fat 17.8g |Total Carbohydrate30.4g|Sugars25.8g|Protein6.6g|Potassium180 mg|Sodium 90 mg
Storage Put into an airtight jar and keep in the refrigerator for up to five days.
Reheat: just defrost at room temperature for a few hours

5.7 Omelettes

Preparation: 10 minutes
Cooking time: 00 minutes
Servings : 4

Ingredients

- Paprika
- Coconut milk -2 tbsp. (30 ml)
- cream cheese -1 tbsp.
- Fresh ground pepper
- Diced onions and bell peppers
- Eggs -2

Preparation

1. Apply nonstick cooking spray to a little nonstick skillet. In a bowl, mix together the eggs, spices, and coconut milk until frothy.
2. After being cooked through in the skillet over medium heat, your peppers and onion should be fully cooked.
3. Place the peppers, onions, and egg mixture on a plate. Tilt the pan to aid in a more equal cooking of the egg mixture. When the cheese has partially set, add it.
4. After the omelette has set, fold it in half and serve it with a slice of toast.

Nutrition Information[per serving]
Calories 175| Fat 12.7g|TotalCarbohydrate 204g|Sugars 0.9g|Protein13.2g|Potassium 215mg|Sodium 168 mg
Storage Put into an airtight jar and keep in the refrigerator for up to five days.
Reheat: just defrost at room temperature for a few hours

5.8 Apple Oatmeal

Preparation: 10 minutes
Cooking time: 00 minutes
Servings : 4

Ingredients

- Apples, - 4
- oats -1 cup(50 g)

- ground cinnamon -½ tsp. (2g)
- non-fat plain Greek yogurt - ½ cup (100 g)
- water - 4 cups (960 ml)
- Coconut sugar, 3tbsp. (45 g)
- salt -¼ tsp. (1 g)

Preparation

1. Remove the core from two apples and shred the fruit using a box grater with large holes.
2. Place a big pan on the fire and turn the heat to medium-high. Oats should be added, then cooked for two minutes while being constantly stirred. The water, apple shreds, and other ingredients should be brought to a boil. Ten minutes of simmering cooking on low heat with frequent stirring.
3. While you wait, chop the remaining 2 apples.
4. After cooking the oats for 10 minutes, add the diced apples, 2 tablespoons of coconut sugar, cinnamon, and salt. Cook the mixture for a further 15 to 20 minutes, stirring periodically, or until the apples are tender and the oatmeal is quite thick. There are four dishes that contain oats. Each dish should have two tablespoons of yoghurt and a third of a teaspoon of coconut sugar.

Nutrition Information[per serving]
Calories 318| Fat 3.4g |Total Carbohydrate65.7g|Sugars8.8g|Protein11.3g|Potassium 446mg|Sodium 57 mg
Storage Put into an airtight jar and keep in the refrigerator for up to five days.
Reheat: just defrost at room temperature for a few hours

5.9 Tofu and Kale scramble

Preparation: 10 minutes
Cooking time: 10 minutes
Servings: 2
Ingredients

- scallions -3
- black pepper - 1 pinch (1/2 g)
- firm tofu - 1 block
- ground turmeric - ½ tsp (2 g)
- kale -5 ounces (140 g)
- olive oil- 2 Tbsp. (30 ml)
- fresh whole basil leaves -½ cup –(3g)
- kosher salt -1 dash
- lemon juice -1 tsp (4 ml)
- cayenne pepper -1/8 tsp (1/2 g)

Preparation

1. Cut the scallions into thin slices and separate the white from the green sections.
2. Chop the basil and kale.
3. After draining, cut the tofu into 1/2-inch pieces.
4. In a larger bowl, mix the tofu with the cayenne, turmeric, 1/4 teaspoon salt, and 1/2 teaspoon black pepper.
5. Combine completely, then set aside.
6. While the oil is cooking, preheat a sizable nonstick skillet over medium-high heat.
7. Add the scallion whites and stir-fry for about a minute, or until they soften.
8. Boil the tofu mixture for about five minutes, stirring often, or until it resembles scrambled eggs and is just starting to turn colour.
9. Stir in the kale, lemon juice, and 1/2 teaspoon salt and continue cooking for about a minute, or until the spinach wilts.
10. Add the scallion greens and cook for about a minute, or until they are just warmed through and starting to soften.
11. Remove the pan from the heat and stir in the basil. Add salt and pepper to taste.

Nutrition Information [per serving]
Calories 215|Fat 16.3g |Total   Carbohydrate 14g| Sugars 3.3g

| Protein7.3g | Potassium728mg | Sodium 123 mg

Storage Put into an airtight jar and keep in the refrigerator for up to five days.

Reheat: just defrost at room temperature for a few hours

5.10 Porridge

Preparation: 10 minutes
Cooking time: 00 minutes
Servings : 4
Ingredients

- dry old-fashioned oats - 1 cup (40 g)
- coconut milk - 2 cups (480 ml)
- chopped walnuts - 1/4 cup (32 g)
- maple syrup - 1 Tbsp. (15 g)
- Apple -1 large

Preparation

1. In a pot, combine milk and oats.
2. Bring the porridge to a boil while stirring occasionally.
3. Lower the heat and cook the oats for a few of seconds, or until they are soft and mushy.
4. Transfer to serving bowls and garnish with maple syrup, banana slices, and almonds.

Nutrition Information[per serving]

Calories 431 | Fat 14.4 g | Total Carbohydrate62.7g | Sugars 28.8g | Protein17.1g | Potassium 221 mg | Sodium 122 mg

Storage Put into an airtight jar and keep in the refrigerator for up to five days.

Reheat: just defrost at room temperature for a few hours

5.11 Energy Bars

Preparation: 10 minutes
Cooking time: 00 minutes
Servings : 8
Ingredients

- honey -3 tbsp. (45 g)
- rolled oats -1 cup (80 g)
- eggs -3 large
- applesauce -1/3 cup (81 g)
- unsalted peanuts, chopped -3 tbsp. (45 g)
- shredded coconut -1/3 cup (27 g)
- ground cinnamon -1/2 tsp. (2 g)

Preparation

1. 325 degrees F (162 C) in the oven. A 9-inch square pan should be coated with frying oil.
2. In a sizable mixing bowl, combine the oats, coconut, chocolate chips, cinnamon, and peanuts.
3. Lightly mash the eggs in a tiny mixing bowl. Add honey and applesauce, and combine well.
4. After adding the egg mixture to the oat mixture, thoroughly combine.
5. Evenly press the ingredients into the bottom of the 9-by-9-inch pan that has been greased.
6. Cook for 40 minutes. Bars should be sliced after cooling.
7. Keep cold in an airtight container for up to a week.

Nutrition Information[per serving]

Calories 125 | Fat 5.3g | TotalCarbohydrate 15.9g | Sugars 8.1g | Protein 4.8g | Potassium 110mg | Sodium 29 mg

Storage Put into an airtight jar and keep in the refrigerator for up to five days.

Reheat: just defrost at room temperature for a few hours

5.12 Blueberry Blast Smoothie

Preparation: 10 minutes

Cooking time: 00 minutes

Servings : 4

Ingredients

- protein powder -6 tbsp. (90 g)
- 8 ice cubes
- Pineapple juice -14 ounces (400 ml)
- Stevia -4 packets
- frozen blueberries -1 cup (145 g)

Preparation

1. Blend each item in the blender until it is smooth.

Nutrition Information[per serving]

Calories 253|Fat 3g|Total Carbohydrate 27.4g|Sugars 88g|Protein 34g|Potassium 420mg|Sodium 85 mg

Storage Put into an airtight jar and keep in the refrigerator for up to five days.

Reheat: just defrost at room temperature for a few hours

5.13 Eccentric Taste

Preparation: 10 minutes

Cooking time: 05 minutes

Servings :1

Ingredients

- ½ sprig rosemary
- Cream cheese-½ tsp. (2 g)
- eggs - 2 large
- chili powder -½ tsp. (2 g)

Preparation

1. Use nonstick oil spray to coat a coffee cup that can go in the microwave.
2. Into the mug, crack the eggs.
3. Add the rosemary, parmesan cheese, and chilli powder.
4. Combine the ingredients.
5. Cook the mug in the microwave for 1-2 minutes at the highest power setting (about 1200 watts). Eat straight out of the cup or deform onto a plate.

Nutrition Information[per serving]

Calories 193|Fat 13.3g|Total Carbohydrate 2.4g|Sugars 0.8g |Protein17.3g|Potassium16 mg|Sodium 283 mg

Storage Put into an airtight jar and keep in the refrigerator for up to five days.

Reheat: just defrost at room temperature for a few hours

5.14 Strawberry mockarita

Preparation: 10 minutes

Cooking time: 00 minutes

Servings : 6

Ingredients

- Strawberries - 4 cups (664g)
- Ice -2 cups
- lime juice -1/4 cup (10 g)
- Water -2 cups –(480 ml)
- Coconut sugar -1/4 cup (25 g)

Preparation

1. Blend the items together in a blender. Until smooth, blend.

Nutrition Information[per serving]

Calories 62|Fat 0.3g|Total Carbohydrate 15.9g|Sugars 13.2g |Protein0.7g|Potassium150mg|Sodium 3 mg

Storage Put into an airtight jar and keep in the refrigerator for up to five days.

Reheat: just defrost at room temperature for a few hours

5.15 Blueberry lavender lemonade

Preparation: 10 minutes

Cooking time: 00 minutes

Servings : 16

Ingredients

- Cold water
- Splenda sweetener -2 tbsp.(30 g)
- lemon juice -1 cup (240 ml)
- Water -2 cups (480 ml)

- granulated sugar -1/4 cup –(50 g)
- Blueberries -16 ounces – (450 g)
- dried lavender flowers -1 tbsp.-(6 g)

Preparation

1. Put aside a 1-gallon pitcher that has been filled with 4 cups of ice. Bring two cups of water to a roaring boil in a medium saucepan. Lavender, sugar, and blueberries must all be added to the pan. Boil the blueberries and sugar until they burst, which should take around 5 minutes.
2. Fill the pitcher with ice, then pour the leftover blueberry mixture over it. Discard the pitcher. Splenda and lemon juice should be added to the pitcher. Cold water ought to be around halfway full. Completely combine.

Nutrition Information[per serving]

Calories 32|Fat 0.2g|Total Carbohydrate 7.6g |Sugars 6.8g|Protein 0.3g|Potassium 41mg|Sodium 4 mg

Storage Put into an airtight jar and keep in the refrigerator for up to five days.

Reheat: just defrost at room temperature for a few hours

Pancakes

Preparation: 10 minutes

Cooking time: 10 minutes

Servings :16

Ingredients

- Eggs -2
- baking soda -1½ tsp. (6g)
- cream of tartar -1 tsp. (4 g)
- strawberry - 2 cups –(304 g)
- applesauce, unsweetened -2 cup (488 g)
- almond flour -2 cups
- canola oil -1 tbsp. (15 ml)
- almond milk -2 cups –(480 ml)

Preparation

1. A skillet or frying pan must be preheated over medium heat.
2. In a bowl, mix the dry ingredients.
3. In a big bowl, mix the wet ingredients. Before adding the dry ingredients, combine all of the wet ingredients.
4. Adding oil to the pan Add the ingredients for the pancakes to the skillet using a measuring cup with a 1/3 cup capacity. Use a spatula to flip the pancakes once bubbles appear. Allow the second side to brown when the middle no longer seems damp.
5. Half a cup of applesauce and half a cup of strawberries go great with pancakes.

Nutrition Information[per serving]

Calories 158|Fat 8.7g |Total   Carbohydrate 17.4g|Sugars   4.8g|Protein3.2g|Potassium 156mg|Sodium 447 mg

Storage Put into an airtight jar and keep in the refrigerator for up to five days.

Reheat: just defrost at room temperature for a few hours

6 SALAD RECIPES

6.1 Garden Salad

Preparation: 10 minutes
Cooking time: 00 minutes
Servings :4

Ingredients

Dressing

- olive oil -½ tbsp.. (7 ml)
- vinegar – 1 tbsp. (15 ml)
- Celery -1stalk
- cucumber – ½
- Romaine lettuce -1½cups (9 g)
- baby carrots -4
- Red onion – ½
- iceberg lettuce -2cups (110 g)

Preparation

1. In a sizable bowl, combine all the vegetables.
2. To make the dressing, combine the vinegar and oil, or use your preferred low-sodium salad dressing.
3. Enjoy!

Nutrition Information[per serving]

Calories 49|Fat 0.4g|Total Carbohydrate 11.4g|Sugars 5.2g|Protein 1.8g|Potassium 416mg|Sodium 60 mg

Storage For three to four days, keep them in the refrigerator in a sealed container.

Reheat: just defrost at room temperature for a few hours

6.2 Chicken Apple Crunch Salad

Preparation: 10 minutes
Cooking time: 00 minutes
Servings :4

Ingredients

- low-fat mayonnaise -1/3 cup (78 g)
- apple -1 cup (100 g)
- black pepper-1/4 tsp. (1g)
- celery -1/2 cup (50 g)
- low-fat sour cream -1 tbsp. (12 g)
- raisins -1/4 cup (49 g)
- cooked chicken -2 cups (280 g)
- cinnamon -1/4 tsp. (1g)
- scallions -2 tbsp. (12 g)
- lemon juice -1 tsp. (4 g)

Preparation

1. Cooked chicken cubes. Juice the apple and celery. Trim scallions.
2. In a sizable salad bowl, mix the raisins, chicken, scallions, celery, and apple.
3. In a bowl, mix the lemon juice, black pepper, cinnamon, mayonnaise, and sour cream. The liquid should then be incorporated with the chicken-apple mixture.
4. Before serving, chill in the refrigerator.

Nutrition Information[per serving]

Calories 237|Fat 9.7g|Total Carbohydrate 16.4g|Sugars10.8g|Protein21.2g|Potassium 280mg|Sodium 197 mg

Storage For up to five days, place the airtight container and store in the fridge.

Reheat: just defrost at room temperature for a few hours

6.3 Lemon Thyme Tuna Pasta Salad

Preparation: 10 minutes
Cooking time: 10 minutes
Servings :2

Ingredients

- lemon juice -2 tbsp. (30 ml)
- shirataki pasta, dry -4 oz (113 g)
- canola oil -1teaspoon (4 ml)

- garlic -⅛tsp, (1/2 g)
- dijon mustard -1½tsp. (6 g)
- chives -4tsp (16 g)
- White Tuna – 2 packs (370 g)
- dried thyme -2tbsp, (12 g)
- dry mustard-⅛tsp, (1/2 g)
- ground black pepper -⅛tsp, (1/2 g)

Preparation

1. Pasta should be prepared as directed on the package, then rinsed and cooled.
2. Add pasta, chives, and lemon thyme after draining the tuna.
3. After carefully blending all the ingredients in a different bowl, spoon the dressing over the spaghetti and tuna combination.
4. Combine everything and garnish with a sprig of lemon thyme.

Nutrition Information[per serving]

Calories 442|Fat 5.1g|Total Carbohydrate 43g|Sugars 2.4g|Protein 54.4g|Potassium 471mg|Sodium 96 mg

Storage For up to five days, place the airtight container and store in the fridge.

Reheat: just defrost at room temperature for a few hours

6.4 Chicken Fruit Salad

Preparation: 10 minutes
Cooking time: 00 minutes
Servings :8

Ingredients

- small shell pasta, uncooked -8 ounces – (226 g)
- seedless grapes -1-1/2 cups (138 g)
- mandarin oranges -15 ounces (425 g)
- celery -1-1/2 cups (152 g)
- cooked chicken -3 cups (420 g)
- mayonnaise -3/4 cup (175 g)

Preparation

1. Chicken cooked in cubes. grapes into halves and slice celery. Drain oranges, mandarins.

2. Do not add salt when cooking pasta per package directions. Drain and chill by rinsing in cold water. Good drainage
3. All ingredients and cooked pasta should be combined in a big bowl. Blend thoroughly.
4. Refrigerate and cover the dish until ready to serve.

Nutrition Information[per serving]

Calories 276| Fat 9.7g|Total Carbohydrate 28.2g|Sugars 8.2g
|Protein19.1g|Potassium 276mg|Sodium 210 mg

Storage For up to five days, place into airtight container and store in the fridge.

Reheat: just defrost at room temperature for a few hours

6.5 Yogurt-Covered Fruit Salad

Preparation: 10 minutes
Cooking time: 00 minutes
Servings :2

Ingredients

- mandarin oranges in light syrup, drained – 4 oz. (113 g)
- Apple -1
- dried cranberries -⅓cup (10 g)
- Strawberries – 6
- Greek yogurt -6oz (170 g)
- green grapes -10
- fresh pineapple chunks -½cup (82 g)

Preparation

1. Strawberry, grape, and apple should all be washed.
2. Make bite-sized apple pieces by chopping it.
3. Strawberry slices
4. Combine yoghurt, dried cranberries, apple, grapes, Mandarin oranges, pineapple, and raisins.
5. For two hours, cover and chill.
6. Serve with strawberry slices as a garnish.

Nutrition Information[per serving]

Calories 195 | Fat 1.7g | Total Carbohydrate 37.4g | Sugars 28g | Protein 9.9g | Potassium 451mg | Sodium 43 mg

Storage For up to five days, place in a airtight container and store in the fridge.

Reheat: just defrost at room temperature for a few hours

6.6 Couscous Salad with Tangy Dressing

Preparation: 10 minutes

Cooking time: 00 minutes

Servings :4

Ingredients

- allspice -1 tsp. (4 g)
- red bell pepper -½cup (75 g)
- Lemons, juiced – 2
- chopped carrots -½cup (60 g)
- chopped yellow bell pepper -½cup (75 g)
- olive oil -1tbsp (15 ml)
- minced garlic -1 tbsp. (15 g)
- whole sugar snap peas -1cup, (35 g)
- couscous, dry -1 cup (173 g)
- frozen corn -½cup (40 g)
- dried oregano leaves -1tsp (4 g)
- cucumbers - 3

Preparation

1. Prepare the couscous and chill according to the directions on the container.
2. In a sizable bowl, combine the couscous that has cooled with the carrots, snow peas, corn, red and yellow peppers, cucumbers, and other veggies.
3. In a small bowl, mix the lemon juice, olive oil, all of the spices, dried oregano, and minced garlic.
4. Serve cold after mixing.

Nutrition Information[per serving]

Calories 273 | Fat 4.5g | Total Carbohydrate 54g | Sugars 7.2g | Protein 8.7g | Potassium 642mg | Sodium 24 mg

Storage For up to five days, place into an airtight container and store in the fridge.

Reheat: just defrost at room temperature for a few hours

6.7 Fruit Salad Slaw

Preparation: 10 minutes

Cooking time:00 minutes

Servings :6

Ingredients

- green cabbage -1/2 cup (45 g)
- red apples -1 cup (170 g)
- carrots -1/4 cup (30 g)
- pineapple juice -3 tbsp. (45 ml)
- coconut sugar -2 tsp. (8 g)
- mayonnaise -1/4 cup (58 g)
- purple cabbage -1/2 cup (45 g)
- crushed pineapple -8 ounces –(226 g)

Preparation

1. unpeeled apples are diced. Grate carrots and cannabe. Remove liquid from pineapple chunks after draining.
2. Thoroughly combine 3 tablespoons of the saved pineapple juice, sugar, and mayonnaise in a another bowl. Set aside.
3. In a medium bowl, mix the pineapple, apples, cabbage, and carrots.
4. the mayonnaise mixture in.
5. Store in the fridge covered until cool.

Nutrition Information[per serving]

Calories 90 | Fat 3.4g | Total Carbohydrate 15.9g | Sugars 4.8g | Protein 0.6g | Potassium 127mg | Sodium 76 mg

Storage For up to five days, place into an airtight container and store in the fridge.

Reheat: just defrost at room temperature for a few hours

6.8 Chicken Salad

Preparation: 10 minutes

Cooking time: 00 minutes

Servings :4

Ingredients

- Gala apples -2
- light mayonnaise -3 tbsp. (45 g)
- grapes -½ cup
- cooked chicken -2 cups
- green onions - 2

Preparation

1. Grapes into halves.
2. Cut up the green onions.
3. Apple cored and chopped.
4. Combine each component.
5. Before serving, give the food an hour to rest in the refrigerator.
6. White bread or low-sodium crackers are both suitable accompaniments to the chicken salad.

Nutrition Information[per serving]

Calories 205|Fat 6.1g|Total Carbohydrate 16.2g|Sugars12.8g|Protein20.2g|Potassium 235mg|Sodium 124 mg

Storage For up to five days, place into airtight container and store in the fridge.

Reheat: just defrost at room temperature for a few hours

6.9 Cucumber Mint Salad

Preparation: 10 minutes

Cooking time: 00 minutes

Servings :4

Ingredients

- Cucumber – 1
- black pepper -1/4 tsp. (1 g)
- fresh mint -2 tbsp. (22 g)
- extra virgin olive oil -2 tsp. (8 ml)
- garlic powder-1/4 tsp. (1 g)

Preparation

1. Fresh mint is chopped while the cucumber is washed and diced. In a bowl, combine the cucumber and mint.
2. Pepper, garlic powder, and olive oil are added. Mix thoroughly.
3. To cool, refrigerate. Before serving, you can add a little vinegar if you like.

Nutrition Information[per serving]

Calories 33|Fat 2.4g |Total Carbohydrate 3.2g|Sugars 1.3g |Protein 0.6g|Potassium 127mg|Sodium 2 mg

Storage For up to five days, place into container and store in the fridge.

Reheat: just defrost at room temperature for a few hours

6.10 Turkey Waldorf Salad

Preparation: 10 minutes

Cooking time: 00 minutes

Servings :6

Ingredients

- red apples -3 medium
- celery -1 cup (100 g)
- apple juice -2 tbsp. –(30 ml)
- turkey breast, cooked -12 ounces (340 g)
- mayonnaise -1/4 cup (58 g)
- onion -1/2 cup (80 g)

Preparation

1. Cut the turkey into pieces. Slice onion, then dice celery and apples.
2. In a medium bowl, mix the turkey, apple, onion, and celery.
3. Include mayonnaise and apple juice. mixing until everything is incorporated.
4. Chill before serving.

Nutrition Information[per serving]

Calories 140|Fat 8.7g|Total Carbohydrate 27.4g|Sugars 20.8g|Protein 17g|Potassium 425 mg|Sodium 124 mg

Storage For up to five days, place into airtight container and store in the fridge.

Reheat: just defrost at room temperature for a few hours

6.11 Cobb Salad

Preparation: 10 minutes
Cooking time: 00 minutes
Servings :2

Ingredients

- roasted turkey, sliced -4 ounces (113 g)
- chives -2 tbsp.(8 g)
- Egg, boiled, -1
- romaine lettuce -2 cups (110 g)
- watercress -1 cup (35 g)
- blue cheese, crumbled -¼ cup (33 g)
- turkey bacon, cooked and chopped -2 slices

Preparation

1. Place all the lettuce in a large basin and toss.
2. Other veggies, meat, and cheese can be added as toppings.
3. Divide the items for your salad's toppings into rows for a traditional presentation.
4. Enjoy!

Nutrition Information[per serving]

Calories 188|Fat 8.7g|Total Carbohydrate 3.3g|Sugars 1.8g|Protein 18.2g|Potassium 244mg|Sodium 563 mg
Storage For up to five days, place into airtight container and store in the fridge.
Reheat: just defrost at room temperature for a few hours

6.12 Pasta Salad

Preparation: 10 minutes
Cooking time: 10 minutes
Servings :4

Ingredients

- cooked fusilli pasta - 2 cups (170 g)
- Red onion – ½
- green bell pepper – ½

- cauliflower – 1 cup (100 g)

Preparation

1. Follow the package's instructions for cooking pasta.
2. Include vegetables.
3. Add your preferred low-fat dressing before tossing.
4. Enjoy!

Nutrition Information[per serving]

Calories 158|Fat 8.7g|Total Carbohydrate 17.4g|Sugars 4.8g |Protein 3.2g|Potassium 156mg|Sodium 447 mg
Storage For up to five days, place the jar's lid on and store in the fridge.
Reheat: just defrost at room temperature for a few hours

6.13 Tuna Pasta Salad

Preparation: 10 minutes
Cooking time: 00 minutes
Servings :4

Ingredients

- celery -1/4 cup (25 g)
- lemon zest -1 tsp. (4 g)
- Italian salad dressing -1/4 cup (30 g)
- green onion -2 tbsp. (12 g)
- low-fat mayonnaise -1/4 cup (58g)
- cooked pasta -2 cups (280 g)
- yellow bell pepper -2 tbsp. (30 g)

Preparation

1. Finely chop the green onion, bell pepper, and celery,
2. Combine lemon zest, bell pepper, onion, cooked pasta, and celery in a mixing bowl.
3. In another bowl, combine the salad dressing and mayonnaise.
1. Drizzle dressing all over the spaghetti mixture in step 4.
4. Include tuna in the spaghetti mixture.
5. Gently mix all of the ingredients together until they are wet and thoroughly mixed.

6. Chill for an hour to allow flavours to combine.
2. Nutrition Information[per serving]

Calories 223| Fat 6.7g|Total Carbohydrate 27.4g|Sugars 4.1g |Protein11.2g|Potassium245 mg|Sodium 239 mg

Storage For up to five days, place into an airtight container and store in the fridge.

Reheat: just defrost at room temperature for a few hours

6.14 Lettuce and Mushroom Salad

Preparation: 10 minutes
Cooking time: 00 minutes
Servings :4

Ingredients

- red onion -1/4 cup (40 g)
- carrots -1/2 cup (61 g)
- Butter head lettuce -3 cups (165 g)
- mushrooms -1 cup (70 g)

Preparation

1. Mince the onion and carrot.
2. Combine the vegetables in a large basin.
3. After being split into four servings, serve in chilled salad bowls.

Nutrition Information[per serving]

Calories 18|Fat 0.2g|Total Carbohydrate 3.4g |Sugars 1.8g|Protein 1.2g|Potassium 208mg|Sodium 13 mg

Storage For up to five days, place into an airtight container and store in the fridge.

Reheat: just defrost at room temperature for a few hours

7 SOUPS & STEWS

7.1 Mushroom Soup

Preparation: 10 minutes
Cooking time: 10 minutes
Servings :6

Ingredients

- garlic -1 clove
- mushrooms -12-ounces (340 g)
- shallots -3 medium (85g)
- celery -2 stalks (80g)
- vegetable stock -4 cups (960 ml)
- fresh thyme -4 cups
- flour -5 tbsp.(75 g)
- Bay leaves -2
- fresh ground black pepper -½ tsp. (2 g)
- coconut oil -3 tbsp. (45 ml)
- Coconut yogurt -½ cup (122 g)

Preparation

1. Heat coconut oil in a big skillet or Dutch oven before beginning to make your kidney-friendly mushroom soup.
2. Include celery, shallots, and freshly ground pepper. On a medium-high heat, sauté.
3. Cook, stirring regularly, for 2 minutes, or until fragrant and browned.
4. Set the thermostat to medium. Add the garlic and simmer for a further two minutes.
5. Add the pieces of mushroom. Stirring frequently, let the mushrooms simmer for 10 minutes or until all of their liquid has disappeared.
6. Sprinkle the flour on top of the ingredients that have been sautéed. Stir and toast over medium heat for one to two minutes.
7. Add one cup of heated stock together with the bay leaves and thyme sprigs. Add the second cup of liquid to the mushroom soup and whisk. Blend thoroughly by stirring.
8. Include the final 2 cups of stock. The mushroom soup needs to thicken for 15 minutes.
9. Take out the thyme and bay leaves.
10. Use an immersion blender in the pot or pour the liquid into a blender.
11. Puree the mixture as smooth as it will allow.If using a blender, pour the mushroom soup back into the pot. Blend well after adding the yoghurt.
12. Cook for four more minutes after bringing to a simmer.
13. With a garnish of herbs or mushroom slices, serve the kidney-friendly mushroom soup.

Nutrition Information[per serving]

Calories 140|Fat 7.3g|Total Carbohydrate 14.7g|Sugars 4.5 g |Protein4.2g|Potassium467mg|Sodium 113 mg

Storage a sealed container is used to store soup for up to 3 -4 days.

Reheat: just defrost at room temperature for a few hours

7.2 Simple Cabbage Soup

Preparation: 20 minutes
Cooking time: 35 minutes
Servings :8

Ingredients

- Chicken stock -1 cup (240 ml)
- fresh thyme -2 tbsp. (8g)
- carrots – 2
- tomatoes -2
- water -6 cups (1440 ml)
- onion – ½
- olive oil -1 tbsp. (15 ml)
- green cabbage – ½ head
- Black pepper, freshly grounded, to taste
- garlic - 2 tsp. (8 g)

25

Preparation

1. In a big pot, heat the olive oil to a medium-high temperature.
2. Sauté the onion and garlic until they are tender, about 3 minutes.
3. While stirring in the water, chicken stock, tomatoes, and cabbage, bring to a boil. The vegetables should simmer for about 30 minutes, or until they are soft, on medium-low heat.
4. Black pepper is used to season the soup. Sprinkled thyme on top; serve hot.

Nutrition Information[per serving]

Calories 45|Fat 2g|Total Carbohydrate 6.7g|Sugars 3.4g|Protein 1.2g|Potassium 220mg|Sodium 113 mg

Storage a sealed container is used to store soup for up to 3 -4 days.

Reheat: just defrost at room temperature for a few hours

7.3 Chicken Wild Rice Asparagus Soup

Preparation: 10 minutes
Cooking time: 20 minutes
Servings :8

Ingredients

- unsalted butter -1/4 cup (56 g)
- nutmeg -1/4 tsp. (1 g)\
- all-purpose flour -1/2 cup (62 g)
- unsweetened almond milk, unenriched -4 cups (960 ml)
- onion -1/2 cup (58 g)
- garlic cloves -3
- long grain and wild rice blend -3/4 cup (138 g)
- fresh ground pepper-1/2 tsp. (2 g)
- asparagus -2 cups (268 g)
- chicken broth -4 cups(960 ml)
- salt -1/2 tsp. (2 g)
- carrots -1 cup (128 g)
- thyme-1/2 tsp. (2 g)

- cooked chicken -2 cups (280 g)
- bay leaf -1

Preparation

1. Prepare the long grain and wild rice mixture in accordance with the directions on the package, but omit the salt and spice packet if one is present.
2. After turning off the heat, continue to cover the rice for an additional 15 minutes. Set aside and let it cool.
3. Cut the onion, carrots, and asparagus into dice. Garlic is sliced.
4. Melt the butter in a Dutch oven and cook the onion and garlic until they are soft. herbs, spices, and carrots. Over medium heat, keep cooking the food until it is soft.
5. After adding the flour, simmer on low heat, stirring often, for about 10 minutes.
6. Include 4 cups of chicken broth and the vermouth. With the aid of a wire whisk, blend until smooth.
7. Cut the cooked chicken into dice. Add the chicken and asparagus to the soup before drizzling the almond milk in gradually. Simmer for 20 minutes.
8. Finish by including the cooked rice.

Nutrition Information[per serving]

Calories 241|Fat 8.9g|Total Carbohydrate 25.4g|Sugars 1.7g|Protein14.2g|Potassium 320mg|Sodium 200 mg

Storage a sealed container is used to store soup for up to 3 -4 days.

Reheat: just defrost at room temperature for a few hours

7.4 Minestrone Soup

Preparation: 15 minutes
Cooking time: 30 minutes
Servings :8

Ingredients

- Olive Oil -2 tbsp. (30 ml)

- Diced Tomatoes, No Salt Added -14-ounce (396 g)
- ground Black Pepper -1 tsp (4 g)
- Basil – Dried -1 tsp (4 g)
- Chicken Broth, Low Fat, Low Sodium – 4 cups (960 ml)
- Garlic -2
- Green Snap Beans, no salt added -1can (260 g)
- Celery stalk -2
- Oregano – Dried -1 tsp (4 g)
- Carrots -1
- chopped Zucchini -½ cup (62 g)
- elbow shaped Macaroni, dry -1½cup (157 g)
- Onion -1/2

Preparation

1. Slice the onion, garlic, and zucchini. shredded carrot Green beans in a can can be cleaned or you can use 1 1/2 cups of freshly cut beans.
2. In a large saucepan or Dutch oven, heat the olive oil over medium-low heat. Add the onions when they are transparent, then simmer for a further 2 to 3 minutes.
3. Include the celery, carrot, zucchini, and garlic. Green beans must be added when using fresh beans. The vegetables should be sautéed for five minutes, or until they are soft.
4. Include black pepper, basil, and canned green beans.
5. Include chicken broth and one can of diced, salt-free tomatoes.
6. After bringing to a boil, simmer. fifteen minutes of cooking.
7. Prepare the pasta as instructed on the package, for 8 to 10 minutes.
8. To finish, add a sprig of fresh basil. After ladling into a bowl, enjoy!

Nutrition Information [per serving]

Calories   178 | Fat   4.6g | Total   Carbohydrate 26g | Sugars   4.3g | Protein   6.7g | Potassium 237mg | Sodium 113 mg

Storage : a sealed container is used to store soup for up to 3 -4 days.

Reheat: just defrost at room temperature for a few hours

7.5 Turkey, Wild Rice and Mushroom Soup

Preparation: 10 minutes

Cooking time: 00 minutes

Servings :4

Ingredients

- turkey, cooked -2 cups (280 g)
- salt -1/2 tsp (2 g)
- carrots -1/2 cup (60 g)
- canned sliced mushrooms -4 ounces (113 g)
- dried thyme -1-1/2 tsp. (6 g)
- black pepper -1/4 tsp.(1 g)
- Bay leaves -2
- olive oil -1 tbsp. (15 ml)
- red bell pepper -1/2 cup (74 g)
- wild rice, uncooked -1/2 cup (80 g)
- low-sodium chicken broth -5 cups (1200 ml)
- Onion -1/2 cup (80 g)
- Original herb seasoning blend -1/4 tsp.(1 g)
- garlic cloves -2

Preparation

1. Finely chop the onion, bell pepper, and carrots. Turkey should be sliced up, with garlic chopped.
2. In a sauce pan over medium heat, bring 1-3/4 cups of stock to a boil before adding the wild rice, which cooks quickly. Simmering at a low to moderate temperature for five minutes, or until the liquid has entirely been absorbed. Set aside.
3. Heat the oil in a Dutch oven over a medium-high flame. Include bell peppers, carrots, onions, and garlic. Sauté in between stirring.

4. Combine the vegetables and the rinsed and drained mushrooms.
5. The remaining 3-1/4 cups of liquid, the turkey, the spice, the thyme, salt, and pepper should all be added to the pan. Cook fully while stirring occasionally.
6. Once the bay leaves have been taken out, add the cooked wild rice to the liquid. Serve immediately.

Nutrition Information[per serving]

Calories 177|Fat 4.9g|Total Carbohydrate 14.7g|Sugars 2g|Protein 18.2g|Potassium 326mg|Sodium 103 mg

Storage a sealed container is used to store soup for up to 3 -4 days.

Reheat: just defrost at room temperature for a few hours

7.6 Rotisserie Chicken Noodle Soup

Preparation: 10 minutes
Cooking time: 20 minutes
Servings :10

Ingredients

- rotisserie chicken -1 prepared (900 g)
- fresh parsley -3 tbsp. (10 g)
- onion -1/2 cup (80 g)
- carrots -1 cup (128 g)
- wide noodles, uncooked -6 ounces (170 g)
- celery -1 cup (101 g)
- low-sodium chicken broth -8 cups (1920 ml)

Preparation

1. Chop the chicken into bite-sized pieces after removing the bones. For the soup, measure 4 cups.
2. Large stockpot with chicken broth added should be brought to a boil.
3. Slice carrots and celery, and chop the onion.
4. To a stockpot, add chicken, veggies, and noodles.

5. Noodles will be ready after around 15 minutes of cooking after bringing to a boil.
6. Add chopped parsley as a garnish.

Nutrition Information[per serving]

Calories 238|Fat 8.2g|Total Carbohydrate 16.8g| Sugars 2.1g
|Protein24.9g|Potassium76mg|Sodium 130 mg

Storage a sealed container is used to store soup for up to 3 -4 days.

Reheat: just defrost at room temperature for a few hours

7.7 Salmon Soup

Preparation: 10 minutes
Cooking time: 10 minutes
Servings :8

Ingredients

- salmon, cooked -1 pound (450 g)
- onion -1/2 cup (80 g)
- black pepper -1/8 tsp. (1/2 g)
- carrot -1 medium
- unsalted butter -2 tbsp. (30 g)
- reduced-sodium chicken broth -2 cups (480 ml)
- coconut milk -2 cups (480 ml)
- water -1/4 cup (60 ml)
- celery -1/2 cup
- cornstarch -1/4 cup (32 g)

Preparation

1. Chop the celery, carrot, and onion.
2. In a 3-quart saucepan, melt the butter over medium-high heat in a stovetop burner. The vegetables should be fork-tender after being cooked in the saucepan.Chunks of precooked salmon should be added to the pan.
3. Add the milk, pepper, and chicken broth while stirring. Mixture should be brought to a boil but not over. Simmer the heat down.

4. Water and cornflour should be combined. Pour gradually into the broth mixture while stirring the soup until it has thickened.
5. For a further five minutes, simmer. Enjoy warm servings!

Nutrition Information[per serving]
Calories158|Fat 7.3g|Total Carbohydrate 8.6g|Sugars 4.1g|Protein 14.2g|Potassium 414mg|Sodium 274 mg

Storage a sealed container is used to store soup for up to 3 -4 days.

Reheat: just defrost at room temperature for a few hours

7.8 Chicken Noodle Soup

Preparation: 10 minutes
Cooking time: 20 minutes
Servings :6
Ingredients
- Ground Oregano- 1/2 tsp (2 g)
- Sliced Carrots - 1 cup (120 g)
- Ground Black Pepper - 1/4 tsp (1 g)
- Chopped Celery - 1/2 cup (50 g)
- Chopped Onions - 1/2 cup (80 g)
- Chicken Stock - 5 cups (1200 ml)
- Ground Basil - 1/2 tsp (2 g)
- Unsalted Butter -1 tbsp. (15 g)
- Egg Noodles, Dry - 2 cups (320 g)
- Chicken Breast, cooked - 8 ounces (226 g)

Preparation
1. Cook all of the chicken first, then slice it into little pieces. And after that, chop all of your vegetables.
2. Melt the butter in a 5-quart Dutch oven over medium heat. It is recommended to sauté onion and celery in butter for 5 minutes, or until they just start to soften. After adding the chicken stock, toss in the chicken, noodles, carrots, basil, oregano, and pepper. boiling point On low heat, simmer for approximately 20 minutes. Serve. There

are 6 parts, each roughly the size of 2 cups.

Nutrition Information[per serving]
Calories 155|Fat 4.5g|Total Carbohydrate 17.2g| Sugars 2.2g |Protein11.2g|Potassiu 278mg|Sodium 103 mg

Storage a sealed container is used to store soup for up to 3 -4 days.

Reheat: just defrost at room temperature for a few hours

7.9 Spring Vegetable Soup

Preparation: 10 minutes
Cooking time: 60 minutes
Servings :5
Ingredients
- frozen corn -1/2 cup (40 g)
- olive oil -2 tbsp. (30 ml)
- dried oregano leaves -1 tsp. (4 g)
- Salt -1/4 tsp. (1 g)
- mushrooms -1/2 cup (35 g)
- garlic powder -1 tsp. (4 g)
- Tomato – 1
- fresh green beans -1 cup (110 g)
- onion -1/2 cup (80 g)
- carrots -1/2 cup (64 g)
- low-sodium vegetable broth -4 cups (960 ml)
- celery -3/4 cup (75 g)

Preparation
1. Green beans should be cut into 2-inch chunks after being trimmed of tips and strings. Dice the tomato, mushrooms, celery, onion, and carrots.
2. Before preparing the celery and onion, preheat the olive oil in a large pot.
3. Bring to a boil after including the other ingredients. 45 to 60 minutes at a simmering temperature.

Nutrition Information[per serving]

Calories 99 | Fat 5.9g | Total Carbohydrate 9.3g | Sugar 2.6g | Protein 3.3g | Potassium 240 mg | Sodium 81 mg

Storage a sealed container is used to store soup for up to 3 -4 days.

Reheat: just defrost at room temperature for a few hours

7.10 Carrot and Apple Soup

Preparation: 10 minutes

Cooking time: 00 minutes

Servings :4

Ingredients

- carrots, -4 large
- ground cinnamon -3 tsp. (12 g)
- olive oil -1 tbsp. (15 ml)
- chickpeas - 8 ounces (226 g)
- fresh ginger -2 tbsp. (30 g)
- white onion, -1 small
- unsweetened almond milk -1.5 cups (360 ml)
- apple – 1
- vegetable broth, no added salt -4 cups (960 ml)

Preparation

1. To warm the olive oil, set a large pot over medium heat. Add the ginger and onion. After around 5 minutes of cooking, an onion should be tender and transparent.
2. Add the broth, applesauce, cinnamon, and carrots.
3. Continue to simmer the soup for a further 15 minutes, or until the veggies are tender.
4. Transfer the soup to a blender after removing it from the heat. Blend after include the almond milk until completely blended. Alternately, mix the vegetables and almond milk in the pot using an immersion blender.

Nutrition Information[per serving]

Calories 369 | Fat 9.9g | Total Carbohydrate 55.4g | Sugars18g | Protein17.2g | Potassium 208mg | Sodium 13 mg

Storage a sealed container is used to store soup for up to 3 -4 days.

Reheat: just defrost at room temperature for a few hours

7.11 Barley Soup

Preparation: 10 minutes

Cooking time: 120 minutes

Servings :8

Ingredients

- turmeric -1 tsp. (4 g)
- vegetable oil -2 tbsp. (30 ml)
- chopped fresh parsley -1/2 cup (30 g)
- tomato paste -1/4 cup (8 g)
- Limes, (1 juiced, 1 sliced into 8 wedges) -2
- chicken stock -2 l
- Carrots -1cup (120 g)
- onion -1
- Coconut cream -1/2 cup (120 g)
- uncooked pearl barley -1 cup (200 g)

Preparation

1. Gently boil the chicken stock in a kettle.
2. Caramelize the onion in the vegetable oil until transparent in a large saucepan over medium heat. Stir the saucepan for one minute after adding the pearl barley. Add pepper, salt, tomato paste, lime juice, and turmeric to the chicken stock while it is still hot. After reaching a rolling boil, the mixture is simmered for an hour.
3. To properly cook the barley and carrots, boil the soup for an additional 30 minutes after adding the carrots. Add a tablespoon at a time of boiling water if the soup is too thick.
4. A small bowl is required to contain the sour cream. Pour 1/2 cup of the hot

soup into the sour cream while stirring continually. Pour the sour cream mixture into the soup pot while continuously whisking. Stir in the parsley leaves.

5. Include fresh lime wedges with the meal.

Nutrition Information[per serving]
Calories 178|Fat 7.4g|Total Carbohydrate 25.4g|Sugars 2.8g|Protein 4.2g|Potassium 218mg|Sodium 130 mg

Storage a sealed container is used to store soup for up to 3 -4 days.

Reheat: just defrost at room temperature for a few hours

7.12 Mushroom barley soup

Preparation: 10 minutes
Cooking time: 20 minutes
Servings :9
Ingredients
- chopped garlic -1/2 tsp. (2 g)
- thinly sliced green onions -1/4 cup (25 g)
- chopped onions -1 1/2 cups (200 g)
- mushrooms -1 cup (70 g)
- vegetable stock -8 cups (1920 ml)
- pearl barley -3/4 cup (150 g)
- canola oil -1 tbsp. (15 ml)
- dry sherry -3 ounces (85 g)
- potato -1/2
- black pepper -1/8 tsp.(1/2 g)
- dried thyme -1 tsp.(4 g)
- carrots -3/4 cup (96 g)

Preparation
1. Heat the oil to medium-high heat in a big stockpot. Thyme, pepper, garlic, onions, and carrots should be added. Sauté the onion for about 5 minutes, or until it becomes translucent.
2. After adding the barley and vegetable stock, bring to a boil. Reduce the heat after the barley has finished cooking,

and let it simmer for about 20 minutes. Potatoes and sherry go well together. The potato should be finished boiling after around 15 minutes. After the meal is over, slice some green onions.

Nutrition Information[per serving]
Calories 111|Fat 1.9g|Total Carbohydrate 18.8g | Sugars 2.3g|Protein 2.8g|Potassium 178mg|Sodium 55 mg

Storage a sealed container is used to store soup for up to 3 -4 days.

Reheat: just defrost at room temperature for a few hours

7.13 Chicken Stew with Mushrooms and Kale

Preparation: 15 minutes
Cooking time: 20 minutes
Servings :4
Ingredients
- Garlic -1
- olive oil -1 tbsp.(15 ml)
- mushrooms, 1 cup (145 g)
- chicken stock -2 cups (480 ml)
- corn starch -1 tbsp. (15 g)
- cooked chicken -2 cups (280 g)
- ground black pepper-1/2 tsp. (2 g)
- Onion -1/4 cup (40 g)
- poultry seasoning -1/2 tbsp. (7 g)
- coconut milk -1/2 cup (120 ml)
- kale -1 cup (67 g)
- red pepper -1/2 cup(68 g)
- garlic powder -1/4 tsp.(1 g)
- paprika -1/2 tsp. (2 g)

Preparation
1. In a big skillet, cook the onions and garlic until the onions are soft and transparent. Once the mushrooms begin to turn brown, add the remaining vegetables and continue to sauté them until they soften.

2. Combine the vegetables with the cooked chicken, chicken stock, and dry spices. Percolate for a time.

3. In a another container, thoroughly combine the milk and cornflour. Stir until thickened, then add to boiling stew.

4. Once the stew has thickened, it is ready to be served. Serve with the type of rice or noodles of your choice.

Nutrition Information[per serving]

Calories 210|Fat 7.1g|Total Carbohydrate 11.1g|Sugars 3.8g|Protein 25.2g|Potassium 439 mg|Sodium 130 mg

Storage a sealed container is used to store soup for up to 3 -4 days.

Reheat: just defrost at room temperature for a few hours

7.14 Chicken Chili Stew

Preparation: 10 minutes
Cooking time: 20 minutes
Servings :4

Ingredients

- cilantro - 2 tbsp. (8 g)
- Red pepper -1
- Carrot -1
- chicken breasts -1lb (450 g)
- ground cumin -½ tsp (2 g)
- frozen corn -1 cup (82 g)
- corn-starch - 1 tbsp. (15 g)
- garlic -4
- freshly ground pepper -¼ tsp (1 g)
- Jalapeno chili -1
- chicken broth -2 ½ cups (600 ml)
- Flour -1 tbsp. (15 g)

Preparation

1. In a large pot, bring 1/4 cup of broth to a boil. until the chicken is white, stirring periodically (about 4-5 minutes). Take out and set aside the chicken.

2. Over medium-high heat, add the garlic and jalapenos to the stock (about 2 minutes). The flour is added after two minutes of stirring at low heat. Gradually pour in 2 cups of broth. Before adding the chicken, red pepper, carrots, corn, pepper, cumin, and cilantro, bring to a boil.On low heat with the lid on, boil the chicken for about 20 minutes, or until it is thoroughly done.

3. Add the stew with the remaining 1/4 cup of stock and cornflour. Cook while stirring often until the food is thoroughly prepared and thickened. Add more cilantro and crushed tortilla chips to the serving dish.

Nutrition Information[per serving]

Calories 308|Fat 9.9g|Total Carbohydrate 15.8g|Sugars 3.8g|Protein 38g|Potassium 628mg|Sodium 113 mg

Storage a sealed container is used to store soup for up to 3 -4 days.

Reheat: just defrost at room temperature for a few hours

7.15 Zucchini-Carrot Soup

Preparation: 10 minutes
Cooking time: 10 minutes
Servings :4

Ingredients

- garlic -2
- carrot -1
- zucchinis - 2
- onion -1 medium
- oat milk -2 cups (480 ml)
- basil -1 tsp (4 g)
- oregano -½ tsp (2 g)
- vegetable broth, no salt added -2 cups (480 ml)

- ground oat flour -3 Tbsp.(45 g)

Preparation

1. The onion and garlic should be cooked until soft in a big saucepan with some water or broth.
2. Bring to a boil while stirring in the milk and broth.
3. Add a few shakes of Mrs. Dash, along with the coarsely mixed oat flour, basil, and oregano.
4. Add carrots and zucchini.
5. When vegetables are soft, reduce heat and simmer for another five minutes.
6. To avoid soup burning, stir it frequently.

Nutrition Information[per serving]

Calories 114|Fat 1.7g|Total Carbohydrate 21.4g|Sugars 12.8g|Protein 3.7g|Potassium 225mg|Sodium 103 mg

Storage a sealed container is used to store soup for up to 3 -4 days.

Reheat: just defrost at room temperature for a few hours

7.16 Cauliflower and Pear Soup

Preparation: 10 minutes
Cooking time: 20 minutes
Servings :8
Ingredients

- Onions -1
- Cider Vinegar -2 Tbsp. (30 ml)
- Pear -2
- Thyme, fresh -6 sprigs
- Carrot -1
- Cauliflower – 1 (850 g)
- Garlic -1 Tbsp. (15 g)
- Cloves, ground -2 tsp (8 g)
- Olive oil -3 Tbsp. (45 ml)
- Vegetable stock -6 cups (1440 ml)
- Apples -3
- Ginger -2 Tbsp. (30 g)
- Honey -¼ cup (84 g)

Preparation

1. Cut the onions and carrots into medium-sized bits as well as the cauliflower into florets. Pears and apples should be peeled and sliced into large pieces.
2. For 10 to 15 minutes, add oil to the skillet and sweat (cook without browning) the veggies and pears.
3. Cider vinegar, ginger, cloves, and vegetable stock should be added. Then, simmer for 15 minutes after bringing to a boil.
4. Thyme should be added, blended, and the texture can be changed by adding more vegetable stock or water.
5. For a wonderful crunch and as a garnish, add croutons.
6. Enjoy!

Nutrition Information[per serving]

Calories 191|Fat 5.9g|Total Carbohydrate 34g|Sugars 24.8g|Protein 3.3g|Potassium 535mg|Sodium 79 mg

Storage a sealed container is used to store soup for up to 3 -4 days.

Reheat: just defrost at room temperature for a few hours

8 VEGETARIAN DISHES

8.1 Eggplant and Tofu Stir-Fry

Preparation: 10 minutes
Cooking time: 10 minutes
Servings :4

Ingredients

- scallions -4
- corn-starch -1 tsp (4 g)
- Garlic -2 cloves
- rice vinegar -3 tbsp. (42 g)
- white rice -1 cup (185 g)
- red serrano or jalapeno pepper -1
- hoisin sauce -2 tbsp. (32 g)
- canola oil -4 tbsp. (60 ml)
- Eggplant -1 small
- fresh basil leaves, torn -1/4 cup (1.5 g)
- Tofu -1 package, 454g,

Preparation

1. Start by cooking the rice as directed on the packet.
2. Preheat a nonstick skillet with one tablespoon of oil. Add the tofu and simmer it for an additional ten minutes, stirring it occasionally. on a platter
3. Include any extra oil. Vegetables should be added and cooked until soft. then include the sauce, tofu, etc. Till the sauce has thickened, toss. the serving dish with rice and basil. Once the stew has thickened, it is ready to be served. Serve with the type of rice or noodles of your choice.

Nutrition Information[per serving]

Calories 520|Fat   24.7g|Total Carbohydrate 55.4g|Sugars   6.2g|Protein   22.9g|Potassium 651mg|Sodium 132 mg

Storage a sealed container is used to store Eggplant and Tofu Stir-Fry for up to 3 -4 days.

Reheat: just defrost at room temperature for a few hours

8.2 Summer zucchini "lasagna"

Preparation: 10 minutes
Cooking time: 15 minutes
Servings :6

Ingredients

- garlic -1 clove
- parmesan cheese, -2 Tbsp (2 oz)
- fresh thyme -3 sprigs
- Zucchini -4
- Pepper to taste
- olive oil -2 tbsp. (30 ml)
- mozzarella cheese –¾ cup (6oz)

Preparation

1. Heat the oven to 350°F (176°C).
2. The zucchini needs to be washed, trimmed, and cut on a mandolin. After adding pepper, set away.
3. Olive oil needs to be heated in a frying pan. Slices of zucchini should be added and sautéed for four minutes, or until just softened.
4. Place a layer of zucchini slices on top of butter on a medium-sized baking sheet. After that, sprinkle some vegan cheese on top.Layer the ingredients alternately for a further layer before adding a top layer of crisscross-patterned zucchini slices. Add freshly chopped thyme and parmesan cheese on top.
5. Cook for 15 minutes on the centre rack, then brown the topping using a high-heat broiler.

Nutrition Information[per serving]

Calories 142|Fat   11.5g|Total Carbohydrate 3.7g|Sugars 1.8g |Protein 7.2g|Potassium 226mg|Sodium 183 mg

Storage a sealed container is used to store Summer zucchini "lasagna" for up to 3 -4 days.

Reheat: just defrost at room temperature for a few hours

8.3 Vegetable and Tofu Stir-Fry

Preparation: 10 minutes
Cooking time: 10 minutes
Servings :4

Ingredients

- tofu -1 package, 454g
- canola oil -1 tbsp. (15 ml)
- bean sprouts -2 cups (368 g)
- carrot -1
- scallions -4
- fresh cilantro -1/4 cup(1 g)
- ginger -1 tbsp. (15 g)
- Rice -1 cup (185 g)
- fresh lime juice -2 tbs.(30 ml)
- hoisin sauce -2 1/2 tbsp. (40 ml)
- bell pepper -1
- roasted peanuts -2 tbsp. (30 g)

Preparation

1. Prepare the rice.
2. A whisk is used to blend lime juice and hoisin sauce.
3. In a big skillet over medium-high heat, warm the oil. Stir-fry the carrot, bell pepper, and ginger for two minutes. Add the bean sprouts and tofu. With frequent tossing, the veggies should be cooked for 3 to 4 minutes. The bean sprouts must be prepared correctly to guarantee food safety.
4. After combining the vegetables with the hoisin sauce mixture, serve them over rice.
5. Add cilantro, peanuts, and scallions on top, if you like..

Nutrition Information[per serving]
Calories 384|Fat 11.9g | Total Carbohydrate55.4g|Sugars

6.7g|Protein18.8g|Potassium208 mg|Sodium 199 mg

Storage a sealed container is used to store Vegetable and Tofu Stir-Fry for up to 3 -4 days.

Reheat: just defrost at room temperature for a few hour

8.4 Zucchini Pancake

Preparation: 10 minutes
Cooking time:10 minutes
Servings :12

Ingredients

- all purpose flour -1 cup (125 g)
- ground cumin-1/2 tsp (2 g)
- almond milk -1/2 cup (120 ml)
- Eggs -3
- Corn -1 cup (164 g)
- black pepper -1/2 tsp (2 g)
- zucchini -2
- baking soda -1 tsp (4 g)
- white sugar -1 tbsp. (15 g)
- cilantro -2 tbsp. (1 g)
- vegetable oil -2 tsp (8 ml)
- Cooking spray

Preparation

1. Blend the following ingredients: eggs, sugar, vegetable oil, milk, flour, and baking soda.
2. Corn, zucchini, and spices are combined.
3. Cooking spray should be used to heat up a skillet over medium heat.
4. About 2 tbsp of batter should be added to the skillet.
5. Cook until both sides are browned.
6. Serve hot.
7. You can make pancakes in advance and reheat them.

Nutrition Information[per serving]
Calories 87|Fat 2.4g|Total Carbohydrate 13.2g|Sugars 2.6g|Protein 3.6g|Potassium 156mg|Sodium 130 mg

Storage a sealed container is used to store Zucchini Pancake or up to 3 -4 days.

Reheat: just defrost at room temperature for a few hours

8.5 Spicy Porcini Mushroom Pasta

Preparation: 10 minutes
Cooking time: 00 minutes
Servings :4

Ingredients

- garlic -2 cloves
- dried sage, - 1/4 tsp (1 g)
- mozzarella cheese -1/2 cup (14 g)
- fresh parsley, chopped -1/3 cup (20 g)
- mushrooms -1 cup (70 g)
- boiling water -1/2 cup (120 ml)
- dried porcini mushrooms-1 small package (30g)
- dried hot chili pepper flakes -1 pinch
- olive oil-1/3 cup (72 ml)
- dried pasta - 2 cups -1/2 pound

Preparation

1. To rehydrate the porcini mushrooms, add 1/2 cup of boiling water.
2. Bring a 3-liter saucepan of water to a boil on the stove for the pasta.
3. In the meantime, prepare the sauce by heating the oil in a large skillet over medium heat. The pan must be large enough to accommodate the cooked noodles.
4. Stir-fry the hot pepper flakes and garlic in the oil until the garlic turns golden.
5. Increase the heat to medium-high, add the white mushrooms, and cook for an additional minute.
6. Cook pasta as stated on the package in boiling water.
7. After pressing the porcini, save the juice and use it to make the sauce.
8. Stir in the chopped porcini.
9. Transfer the soaking liquid into the pan using a fine sieve.
10. Cook for 5 minutes after adding the sage.
11. Do not rinse the pasta after draining; instead, put it hot into the skillet with the mushroom sauce.
12. Serve after adding parsley and boconcini cheese.

Nutrition Information[per serving]
Calories 234│Fat 18.7g│Total Carbohydrate 12.7g│Sugars 0.8g│Protein 5.6g│Potassium 93mg│Sodium 110 mg

Storage a sealed container is used to store Spicy Porcini Mushroom Pasta for up to 3 -4 days.

Reheat: just defrost at room temperature for a few hours

8.6 Fresh Basil Pesto with Pasta

Preparation: 10 minutes
Cooking time: 10 minutes
Servings :4

Ingredients

- Quinoa pasta -2 1/2 cups cooked(-375 grams)
- pine nuts -1/4 cup (34 g)
- Parmesan cheese -1/4 cup (6 g)
- garlic -2 cloves
- olive oil -1/3 cup (72 ml)
- fresh basil -2 cups (12 g)

Preparation

1. Prepare the pasta as directed on the packet.
2. Finely chop the pine nuts, basil, and garlic. Combine everything, and then sprinkle Parmesan on top. including the oil
3. Place fresh pasta on top.
4. Additionally, you can combine basil, Parmesan cheese, and pine nuts in a food processor. Oil should be added while the motor is running. after which, stir in the garlic.

Nutrition Information[per serving]

Calories 326 | Fat 25.9g | Total Carbohydrate 22.4g | Sugars 0.4g | Protein 4.2g | Potassium 132mg | Sodium 130 mg

Storage a sealed container is used to store Fresh Basil Pesto with Pasta for up to 3 -4 days.

Reheat: just defrost at room temperature for a few hours

8.7 Eggplant & Chickpea Curry

Preparation: 20 minutes

Cooking time: 50 minutes

Servings :6

Ingredients

- garam masala -4 tsp (16 g)
- chickpeas, - 1 can (540 ml)
- curry leaves -10-12
- vegetable broth – 1 cup (240 mL)
- dried chillies -2
- sunflower oil -2 tbsp. (30 ml)
- ground coriander -2 tsp (8 g)
- Tomatoes -3
- Eggplants -2 small
- garam masala -4 tsp (16 g)
- black mustard seeds -1 tbsp (15 g)
- turmeric-2 tsp (8 g)
- coconut yogurt – ¾ cup (200 ml)
- onions -2

Preparation

1. Divide each half of the eggplant into wedges after cutting it in half. Half of the eggplants should be sautéed in a large, ideally nonstick skillet with 1/2 tbsp oil for 2-3 minutes on each side, or until they are crisp and golden brown all over. Repeat the procedure with extra oil and the remaining eggplants, place them on a tray, and then set everything aside while you cook the remaining eggplants. Add the remaining oil to the pan along with the mustard seeds and curry leaves. 30 seconds of cooking time or until

aromatic. When the onions are tender and starting to brown, stir them in and continue cooking. After one minute, add the spices and dried chiles along with a dollop of the thick yoghurt. Tomatoes, vegetable broth, and the leftover yoghurt are all added. Simmer until thick and saucy, about 25 to 30 minutes.

2. Add the eggplant and chickpeas by stirring. Once everything is hot and the eggplants are soft, simmer for another 5 minutes or so. If desired, serve the curry with warm naan bread that has been sizzled in a little oil and topped with more curry leaves.

Nutrition Information[per serving]

Calories 400 | Fat 10.9g | Total Carbohydrate 55.4g | Sugars 15g | Protein 52.2g | Potassium 208mg | Sodium 103 mg

Storage a sealed container is used to store Eggplant & Chickpea Curry for up to 3 -4 days.

Reheat: just defrost at room temperature for a few hours

8.8 Sweet Crustless Quiche

Preparation: 10 minutes

Cooking time: 20 minutes

Servings :6

Ingredients

Basic Crustless Quiche:

- Coconut milk -1 cup (250 ml)
- Eggs -3
- Flour -1/2 cup (125 g)

Sweet filling:

- brown sugar -2 tbsp. (30 g)
- Butter -1/4 cup (56 g)
- apples -3

Preparation

1. Eggs, milk, and flour should all be combined in a bowl. Stir until most

lumps are gone. Season with salt and pepper, if preferred.

2. Remark: You might bake this mixture and serve it by itself.

3. For 18 minutes, or until the filling is thoroughly cooked and bubbling, simmer the filling ingredients in a skillet over medium heat.

4. Lightly coat an 8-inch cake pan or a deep-dish pie plate with cooking spray to prevent the quiche from sticking. In the buttered baking dish, evenly spread 3 cups of the prepared filling. When the top is golden brown and a knife put into the centre comes out clean, add the crustless quiche filling and bake for 42 minutes at 350 degrees.

Nutrition Information[per serving]

Calories   231 | Fat   11.3g | Total Carbohydrate28.5g | Sugars16.8g | Protein5.9g | Potassium 195mg | Sodium 111 mg

Storage a sealed container is used to store soup for up to 3 -4 days.

Reheat: just defrost at room temperature for a few hours

8.9 Roasted Spaghetti Squash With Kale

Preparation: 10 minutes
Cooking time: 10 minutes
Servings :6

Ingredients

- bunch kale -1 large (85 g)
- spaghetti squash -1 large
- red chili flakes -½ tsp (2 g)
- Parmesan cheese -½ cup (14 g)
- oregano leaves -2 tsp (8 g)
- olive oil – 2tbsp. (30 ml)
- garlic -2

Preparation

1. 350°F (176 °C)for the oven's temperature.

2. The spaghetti squash should be cut in half lengthwise. Remove the seeds with a big spoon and discard them.

3. Spread 2 tablespoons of extra virgin olive oil over the spaghetti squash and place it on a baking sheet with a rim. Garlic, oregano, and red pepper flakes should all be used. Flip them over so the sliced side is facing up (this will enable them to cook faster). Fork penetration of the squash's flesh requires about 45 minutes of baking in the centre of the oven. Allow it to cool for around five minutes. Squash fibres should be separated from squash halves using a large scoop and fork, then put in a big dish. Till the strands resemble spaghetti, gently toss them.

4. After washing the kale, remove the stems and throw them away. Slice the leaves into big, flavorful bits (about 1 inch). Use a salad spinner to completely dry. The greens should be put in a big basin. Use the remaining 1 teaspoon of olive oil alone to sparingly drizzle it over the leaves. Put the leaves in two rimmed baking pans and distribute them evenly. Roast the leaves for 13 minutes, or until they are crisp and bright green. Place aside.

5. Arrange the spaghetti squash on a large platter and top with the kale chips. To taste, add a pinch of parmesan and salt & pepper.

Nutrition Information[per serving]

Calories 58 | Fat   5.2g | Total Carbohydrate 2.2g | Sugars 18g | Protein 1.2g | Potassium 82 mg | Sodium 221 mg

Storage a sealed container is used to store Roasted Spaghetti Squash with Kale for up to 3 -4 days.

Reheat: just defrost at room temperature for a few hours

8.10 Red Lentil Dahl

Preparation: 10 minutes
Cooking time: 20 minutes
Servings :4
Ingredients

- kosher salt -1/4 tsp (1 g)
- Onion -1 cup (160 g)
- tomato -1
- canola oil -1 tbsp. (15 ml)
- chopped cilantro leaves for garnish
- cinnamon 1 tsp (4 g)
- green chilli pepper- 1
- ground cardamom-1/2 tsp (2 g)
- garlic cloves -4
- red lentils -1 cup (192 g)
- ground turmeric-1/2 tsp (2 g)
- paprika -1/2 tsp (2 g)
- Juice of one half a lemon
- cumin seeds -1/2 tsp (2 g)
- ginger root -1 tbsp. (15 g)

Preparation

1. Before going to bed, soak the lentils in a basin of water for at least 12 hours.
2. After that, rinse the legumes and discard the now-potassium-rich soaking water.
3. Fill a medium pot with 3 cups of room temperature water and the rinsed lentils. Lentils should simmer for 20 minutes on medium heat.
4. To prepare the seasonings:
5. In a medium skillet set over medium heat, warm the oil. To release their aroma, cumin seeds and cinnamon powder should be cooked for 60 to 90 seconds.
6. Add the ginger, garlic, onion, and green chilli pepper at this point. Cook the onions for a further 4 to 6 minutes when they become translucent.
7. Add the tomato, paprika, cardamom, turmeric, salt, and other ingredients to the pan. The tomato should be cooked for 2 to 3 minutes, or until it starts to break apart. After using the cinnamon stick, throw it away.
8. After the lentils have been cooked, remove any extra water. Stir in the hot onion mixture with the lentils in the stew. After adding the lemon juice, mix everything well.
9. Add cilantro as a garnish and serve over basmati rice.

Nutrition Information[per serving]
Calories 233 | Fat 4.3g | Total Carbohydrate 36.4g | Sugars 3.5g | Protein13.2g | Potassium 63mg | Sodium 153 mg
Storage a sealed container is used to store Red Lentil Dahl for up to 3 -4 days.
Reheat: just defrost at room temperature for a few hours

8.11 Garlicky Penne Pasta with Asparagus

Preparation: 10 minutes
Cooking time: 10 minutes
Servings :6
Ingredients

- Butter -2 tbsp. (30 g)
- olive oil -2 tbsp. (30 ml)
- Parmesan cheese - 1/4 cup (7 g)
- lemon juice -2 tsp. (8 ml)
- garlic- 6 cloves
- asparagus -1 pound (450 g)
- red pepper flakes -1/8 tsp.(1/2 g)
- black peper -1/2 tsp.(2 g)
- whole wheat penne pasta, uncooked -8 ounces (226 g)
- hot sauce -1/4 tsp.(1 g)

Preparation
1. Make sure to cook the pasta without salt, following the directions on the package.

2. Trim the asparagus ends to a length of 2 inches. minced garlic
3. Melt the butter and oil in a medium skillet over medium heat. Cook for another 1-2 minutes after adding the garlic and red pepper flakes.
4. Toss the asparagus with the Tabasco sauce, lemon juice, and black pepper in a skillet. It takes 6 minutes to cook asparagus from crisp to tender.
5. After draining, place the spaghetti in a bowl. Throw the asparagus in.
6. Add cheese shavings before serving.

Nutrition Information[per serving]

Calories 234|Fat 10.9g|Total Carbohydrate 30.7g|Sugars 1.8g|Protein 8.3g|Potassium 171mg|Sodium 60 mg

Storage a sealed container is used to store Garlicky Penne Pasta with Asparagus for up to 3 -4 days.

Reheat: just defrost at room temperature for a few hours

8.12 Tempeh Pita Sandwiches

Preparation: 10 minutes

Cooking time: 05 minutes

Servings :4

Ingredients

- Tempeh -8 ounces (226 g)
- balsamic vinegar-2 tbsp.(30 ml)
- onion -1 small
- sesame oil -2 tbsp.(30 ml)
- mayonnaise -4 tsp.(16 g)
- pita bread, 6-inch size -2 pieces
- Red bell pepper -1
- Mushrooms -1/2 cup (35 g)

Preparation

1. Cut the tempeh into 12 equal pieces. Onion, bell pepper, and mushrooms should all be thinly cut.
2. In a big skillet, warm 1 tablespoon of the sesame oil over medium heat. Slices of tempeh may now be added and cooked for an additional 3 to 4

minutes, or until browned, on each side. After adding balsamic vinegar, the item should cook for one minute without being turned. From the pan, take out the tempeh.

3. Heat the remaining sesame oil in the skillet over medium heat. Cook the bell pepper, onion, and mushrooms until they are tender.
4. Cut the pocket after slicing the pita in half. Use a spoon to spread mayonnaise on both sides. Each pita half should include three pieces of tempeh and one-fourth of the veggie mixture. Serve right away.

Nutrition Information[per serving]

Calories 291|Fat 15.1g|Total Carbohydrate 25.4g|Sugars 3.1g|Protein 14g|Potassium 385mg|Sodium 103 mg

Storage a sealed container is used to store Tempeh Pita Sandwiches for up to 3 -4 days.

Reheat: just defrost at room temperature for a few hours

8.13 Pasta Primavera

Preparation: 10 minutes

Cooking time: 10 minutes

Servings :6

Ingredients

- pasta, uncooked -12 ounces (340 g)
- low-sodium chicken broth - 14 ounces(400 ml)
- garlic powder -1/4 tsp.(1 g)
- half & half creamer -1/4 cup (15 g)
- Parmesan cheese -1/4 cup (7 g)
- all-purpose white flour -2 tbsp. (30 g)
- frozen mixed vegetables-12 ounces (340 g)

Preparation

1. In separate pots, prepare the pasta and veggies as directed on the package, but without adding salt. Drain.

2. A medium-sized stockpot should be filled with low-sodium chicken broth and heated gently.

3. While vigorously mixing the flour into the broth, clumps should be avoided.

4. Add the half-and-half and garlic powder.

5. Simmer the mixture over low heat for five to ten minutes, or until it begins to slightly thicken. Sometimes stirring is used when simmering.

6. Include cooked vegetables and spaghetti. Cook until well heated.

7. Sprinkle on some Parmesan cheese before serving.

Nutrition Information

Calories 219 | Fat 1.9g | Total Carbohydrate 40.9g | Sugars 1.8g
| Protein9.3g | Potassium208mg | Sodium 13 mg
Storage a sealed container is used to store Pasta Primavera for up to 3 -4 days.

Reheat: just defrost at room temperature for a few hours

8.14 Vegetarian Red Beans and Rice

Preparation: 10 minutes
Cooking time: 02 hr.30 minutes
Servings :12

Ingredients

- onion – 1
- white rice dry -2 cups (280 g)
- Bay leaves -2
- garlic -4 cloves
- Celery stalks -1
- smoked paprika -2 tsp (8 g)
- black pepper -1/2 tsp (2 g)
- red wine vinegar -1 tbsp. (15 ml)
- unsalted butter 3 tbsp. (45 g)
- dried thyme -2 tsp (8 g)
- Chipotles in adobo sauce -2
- Salt -3/4 tsp (3 g)
- cayenne pepper -1/8 tsp (1/2 g)
- green onions -1 bunch
- dried red beans -1 lb (450 g)

Preparation

1. Let the beans soak all night. The dried beans should be mixed with 2 quarts (8 cups) of water. The soak shouldn't take more than 24 hours. raising beans

2. Melt the butter in a Dutch oven or big soup pot. Along with the onion, bell pepper, and celery, add 1/2 teaspoon of salt. Cooking time for the vegetables should be around 7 minutes, or until they are soft.

3. Paprika, chipotles, bay leaves, cayenne, black pepper, and cayenne pepper are additional seasonings to add. Cook until aromatic, which takes around 30 seconds.

4. Bring 9 cups of water and the beans to a boil. Reduce the heat to low and vigorously simmer for 45 minutes, or until the liquid thickens.

5. Include the remaining 1/4 teaspoon each of salt and vinegar. For thickening and richness, simmer for a further 30 minutes.

6. While you wait, make the rice according to the packet's instructions. Do not add salt, butter, or oil in order for the nutritional content to match what is described here.

7. Top 1/2 cup of beans with 1/2 cup of cooked rice. Every dinner must have green onions!

Nutrition Information[per serving]

Calories 169 | Fat 3.6 g | Total Carbohydrate 25.4g | Sugars 0.8g | Protein 9.5g | Potassium 74mg | Sodium 130 mg
Storage a sealed container is used to store Vegetarian Red Beans and Rice for up to 3 -4 days.

Reheat: just defrost at room temperature for a few hour

9 VEGAN RECIPES

9.1 Parmesan roasted cauliflower

Preparation: 10 minutes
Cooking time: 10 minutes
Servings :6

Ingredients

- Parmesan cheese -1/4 cup (7g)
- lemon zest -1 tsp.(4g)
- kosher salt-1/4 tsp. (1 g)
- fresh basil-1 tsp.(4g)
- cauliflower florets -3 cups (300 g)
- olive oil -2 tbsp. (30 ml)
- paprika -1/4 tsp. (1 g)
- panko bread crumbs -1/2 cup (54 g)

Preparation

1. 1. In a medium-sized pot, bring some water to a boil. The oven is set to 375 degrees (190 C). Spray cooking spray in an 8 by 8 baking dish sparingly.
2. 2. Combine the bread crumbs, cheese, oil, lemon zest, basil, paprika, and salt in a another bowl. The components should be well combined using your hands.
3. Drain the cauliflower from the boiling water after three minutes. Spread the bread crumbs out evenly over the cauliflower once it has been put in the baking dish. After baking for around 15 minutes, the crust should be just browned.

Nutrition Information[per serving]

Calories 92|Fat 5.4g|Total Carbohydrate 8.6g|Sugars 1.6g|Protein 2.1g|Potassium 21mg|Sodium 183 mg

Storage a sealed container is used to store Parmesan roasted cauliflower for up to 3 -4 days.

Reheat: just defrost at room temperature for a few hours

9.2 Lemon rice with golden raisins and almonds

Preparation: 10 minutes
Cooking time: 15 minutes
Servings :8

Ingredients

- olive oil -1 tbsp.(15 ml)
- uncooked brown rice -1 cup (190 g)
- lemon juice -3 tbsp. (45 ml)
- unsalted vegetable broth -1 3/4 cup (420 ml)
- frozen peas -1/2 cup (40 g)
- onions -1/4 cup (40 g)
- ground cinnamon -1/2 tsp.(2 g)
- Almonds -1/2 cup (48 g)
- water -1/3 cup (80 ml)
- ground nutmeg -1/4 tsp. (1 g)
- lemon zest -2 tsp.(8 g)
- golden raisins -1/2 cup (72 g)
- maple syrup -2 tbsp. (30 ml)

Preparation

1. A 325 F oven temperature (162 C). On a baking sheet, sparingly apply cooking spray.
2. Spread the almonds out on the baking sheet in a single layer. When fragrant and browned, bake for about 10 minutes, stirring once or twice. Right away transfer to a plate to chill.
3. Stir the rice, broth, lemon juice and zest, onion, cinnamon, nutmeg, and oil in a medium saucepan set over medium heat. Cook the pot with the lid on for 30 minutes, stirring occasionally, or until the liquid has been absorbed.
4. Combine the water and raisins in a small pot. Having simmered for five minutes while being covered. The peas

should be added and cooked for a further minute. Add the liquid to the rice and cook for a further 15 to 20 minutes, or until all of the liquid has been absorbed.

5. Spoon the rice mixture onto a serving tray when it has been fluffed. Add some maple syrup and roasted almonds as a garnish. Serve right away.

Nutrition Information[per serving]
Calories 183|Fat 4.1g|Total Carbohydrate 33.2g|Total Sugars 10.8g|Protein 5g|Potassium 248mg|Sodium 173 mg
Storage a sealed container is used to store Lemon rice with golden raisins and almonds for up to 3 -4 days.
Reheat: just defrost at room temperature for a few hours

9.3 Maple syrup sage carrots

Preparation: 10 minutes
Cooking time: 10 minutes
Servings :4
Ingredients

- chopped fresh sage -1 tbsp. (2 g)
- ground black pepper -1/4 tsp.(1 g)
- Maple syrup -2 tbsp. (30 ml)
- carrots -2 cups (128 g)
- butter -2 tsp. (8 g)
- salt -1/8 tsp. (1/2 g)

Preparation

1. In a medium-sized pot, bring some water to a boil. Boil for about 5 minutes, or until the carrots are tender to the fork. Drain, and then separate. A medium saute pan should be butter-filled and heated. Once the skillet is hot and the butter has melted, you should add the carrots, maple syrup, sage, pepper, and salt. Approximately 3 minutes of continuous stirring during sautéing. After removing from heat, serve.

Nutrition Information[per serving]
Calories 73|Fat 2g|Total Carbohydrate 14.4g |Sugars 11.8g|Protein 0.6g|Potassium 189mg|Sodium 126 mg
Storage a sealed container is used to store Maple syrup sage carrots for up to 3 -4 days.
Reheat: just defrost at room temperature for a few hours

9.4 Cranberry pecan rice pilaf

Preparation: 10 minutes
Cooking time: 10 minutes
Servings :6
Ingredients

- chopped celery -3/4 cup (75 g)
- kosher salt -1/2 tsp. (2 g)
- chopped onion -1 cup (160 g)
- chopped pecans -1/2 cup (62 g)
- fresh thyme leaves -1 tbsp. (2 g)
- cooked brown basmati rice -2 cups (370 g)
- olive oil -1 1/2 tsp.(6 ml)
- dried cranberries -1/2 cup (28 g)

Preparation

1. A sizable non-stick frying pan should be heated to medium. Sauté the onion and celery after adding the olive oil. Add the cooked rice, pecans, cranberries, salt, and thyme after the vegetables are soft and tender. Mix thoroughly after it has warmed up.

Nutrition Information[per serving]
Calories 323|Fat 9g|Total Carbohydrate 54.1g|Sugars 1.8g|Protein 5.9g|Potassium 194mg|Sodium 208 mg
Storage a sealed container is used to store Cranberry pecan rice pilaf for up to 3 -4 days.
Reheat: just defrost at room temperature for a few hours

9.5 Broccoli with garlic and lemon

Preparation: 10 minutes

Cooking time: 10 minutes

Servings :4

Ingredients

- lemon zest -1 tsp.(4 g)
- kosher salt -1/4 tsp.(1 g)
- minced garlic -1 tbsp.(15 g)
- ground black pepper-1/4 tsp.(1 g)
- olive oil -1 tsp. (4 g)
- broccoli florets -4 cups (364 g)

Preparation

1. Bring one cup of water to a boil in a small saucepan. Cook the broccoli for three minutes in the boiling water, or until it reaches the desired tenderness. broccoli-infused water.
2. Oil should be heated over medium heat in a small sauté pan. Saute the garlic for 30 seconds after adding it. Broccoli, pepper, salt, and lemon zest are suggested ingredients. Plate the mixture when it has been combined.

Nutrition Information[per serving]

Calories 45|Fat 1.5g|Total Carbohydrate 6.9g|Sugars 1.6g|Protein 2.7g|Potassium 300 mg|Sodium 173 mg

Storage a sealed container is used to store Broccoli with garlic and lemon for up to 3 -4 days.

Reheat: just defrost at room temperature for a few hours

9.6 Vegan Fettuccine Alfredo

Preparation: 10 minutes

Cooking time: 10 minutes

Servings :6

Ingredients

- low sodium white beans -15 oz. (425 g)
- onion, diced -½ medium
- garlic, minced - 4 cloves
- whole wheat pasta -8 oz. (226 g)
- Basil dried - 2 tbsp. (10 g)
- rice milk -1 ¾ cups (420 ml)
- frozen baby peas - 2 cups (290 g)

Preparation

1. Don't salt the pasta water while cooking the pasta per the directions on the package.
2. Fill a strainer big enough to fit the cooked pasta over the frozen peas with the frozen peas.
3. Strain the pasta by covering the peas with boiling water after the pasta has finished cooking.
4. On medium heat, add the oil and diced onions to a sizable frying pan. The onions should be sautéed until transparent. Cook for a further minute after adding the garlic. Basil and rice milk are then added. Simmer for three to four minutes.
5. White beans are mashed and added to the pan. Cook for an additional two minutes after stirring to incorporate the beans into the rice milk.
6. Mix in the pasta and peas. After removing from the heat, let the food sit for a while. The sauce thickens and adheres to the pasta as a result of cooling. Before serving, stir.
7. Enjoy!

Nutrition Information [per serving]

Calories 239|Fat 1.9g|Total Carbohydrate 48g|Sugars 5.8g|Protein 8.8g|Potassium 208mg|Sodium 39 mg

Storage a sealed container is used to store Vegan Fettuccine Alfredo for up to 3 -4 days.

Reheat: just defrost at room temperature for a few hours

9.7 Southwest Grain Bowl

Preparation: 10 minutes

Cooking time: 10 minutes

Servings :6

Ingredients

- green pepper - ¼
- black beans, rinsed and drained -15 oz. (425 g)
- red pepper - ¼
- hemp seeds - 2 tsp (8 g)
- cooked quinoa - 2 cups (340 g)
- Southwest Dressing - 1 batch
- Cilantro - 4 tsp (16 g)
- celery, chopped - 1 stalk
- cooked brown rice - 2 cups (380 g)
- Green onion -1

Preparation

1. Start by putting the rice and quinoa in the first of six dishes with the ingredients. 1/3 cup rice and 1/3 cup quinoa will be included in each dish.
2. Distribute the beans, celery, peppers, green onions, and chopped cilantro equally among the six dishes.
3. Delay adding the dressing if you are constructing these bowls ahead of time.
4. If serving right away, top each bowl with 1.5 teaspoons of the Southwest Dressing.
5. Enjoy!

Nutrition Information[per serving]

Calories 540|Fat 5.9g |Total Carbohydrate 140.9g|Sugars 0.8 g|Protein 19.3g|Potassium 208mg|Sodium 9 mg

Storage a sealed container is used to store Southwest Grain Bowl for up to 3 -4 days.

Reheat: just defrost at room temperature for a few hours

9.8 Roasted Cauliflower, Carrots & Onions

Preparation: 10 minutes

Cooking time: 40 minutes

Servings :2

Ingredients

- Carrots -2
- Cauliflower -½ head
- Onion -1
- olive oil - 1 tbsp. (15 ml)

Preparation

1. Warm the oven to 350° Fahrenheit (176 C).
2. Place the cauliflower, carrots, and onion in a single layer on a big baking sheet.
3. Pour some oil over the meal and toss to coat.
4. Roasting for 40 minutes in the oven, tossing halfway through.

Nutrition Information[per serving]

Calories124|Fat 7.1g|Total Carbohydrate 14.9g|Total Sugars 6.8g|Protein 2.4g|Potassium 476mg|Sodium 64 mg

Storage a sealed container is used to store Roasted Cauliflower, Carrots & Onions for up to 3 -4 days.

Reheat: just defrost at room temperature for a few hours

9.9 Tofu Fingers

Preparation: 10 minutes

Cooking time: 10 minutes

Servings :3

Ingredients

- firm tofu -1 ½ cups (340 g)
- seasoning (garlic powder, curry, paprika or other spice) -1 tsp (4 g)
- tamari sauce -1 tsp (4 ml)
- cornflake crumbs -½ cup (14 g)
- water -2 tbsp. (30 ml)

Preparation

1. In a small bowl, combine the tamari and water.
2. Combine the spices and cornflakes crumbs in a separate bowl.
3. Before coating the tofu with the spice mixture, tamari should be added.
4. You must spread out the tofu slices on a baking sheet and lightly oil them.

5. Cook for 20 minutes at 350°F (176°C), flipping once to brown both sides.

Nutrition Information[per serving]

Calories 109|Fat 5.3g|Total Carbohydrate 7.1g|Sugars 1.3g|Protein 10.9g|Potassium 191mg|Sodium 113 mg

Storage a sealed container is used to store Tofu Fingers for up to 3 -4 days.

Reheat: just defrost at room temperature for a few hours

9.10 Pinto Beans

Preparation: 10 minutes

Cooking time: 10 minutes

Servings :6

Ingredients

- white onion - ¼ small
- dry pinto beans -2 cups (386 g)
- water - 8 cups (1920 ml)
- garlic - 2 cloves
- kosher salt - 1 ½ tsp (6 g)
- garlic powder - ½ tbsp. (7 g)

Preparation

1. Clean two cups of beans.
2. Beans, 5 cups of water, 2 garlic cloves, and 1 small onion should all be brought to a boil. Boil for 1 1/2 hours with the lid on over a medium-low heat.
3. Add kosher salt, 3 more cups of water, and garlic powder. For 15 minutes, cook covered.
4. Enjoy with chopped fresh onions, tomatoes, and cilantro on top!

Nutrition Information[per serving]

Calories 228|Fat 0.8g|Total Carbohydrate 41.9g|Sugars 1.8g |Protein 9.3g|Potassium 208mg|Sodium 13 mg

Storage a sealed container is used to store Pinto Beans for up to 3 -4 days.

Reheat: just defrost at room temperature for a few hours

10SIDES AND SMALL PLATES

1.1 Low Salt Macaroni and Cheese

Preparation: 10 minutes
Cooking time: 10 minutes
Servings :4

Ingredients

- grated cheddar cheese -1/2 cup (56 g)
- margarine or salt free butter -1 tsp. (4 g)
- boiling water -2 to 3 cups (480 ml-720 ml)
- dried mustard -1/4 tsp.(1 g)
- noodles, (any shape you want) -2 cups (320 g)

Preparation

1. Water should be at a rolling boil when the noodles are added.
2. Drain.
3. Sprinkle cheese on top while still very hot, then combine butter and mustard.

Nutrition Information[per serving]

Calories 141 | Fat 5.8g | Total Carbohydrate 16.9g | Sugars 0.3g | Protein 5.3g | Potassium 38m | Sodium 85 mg
Storage a sealed container is used to store Low Salt Macaroni and Cheese for up to 3 -4 days.
Reheat: just defrost at room temperature for a few hours

10.1 Pineapple Coleslaw

Preparation: 10 minutes
Cooking time: 00 minutes
Servings :4

Ingredients

- crushed unsweetened pineapple, drained -1 (8 oz) can (226 g)
- shredded cabbage -2 cups (140 g)
- Dash of pepper (optional)
- chopped onion -1/4 cup (40 g)
- Miracle Whip -1/4 cup (59 g)

Preparation

1. Combine each component.
2. Refrigerate for at least an hour before serving.

Nutrition Information[per serving]

Calories 97 | Fat 5g | Total Carbohydrate 13.9g | Sugars 7.8g | Protein 1g | Potassium 134mg | Sodium 113 mg
Storage a sealed container is used to store Pineapple Coleslaw for up to 3 -4 days.
Reheat: just defrost at room temperature for a few hours

10.2 Grilled Cauliflower Wedges

Preparation: 10 minutes
Cooking time: 10 minutes
Servings :8

Ingredients

- olive oil -2 tbsp. (30 ml)
- Optional: Lemon juice, additional olive oil and pomegranate seeds
- Cauliflower -1
- crushed red pepper flakes -1/2 tsp.(2 g)
- ground turmeric -1 tsp (4 g)

Preparation

1. Remove the leaves and trim the cauliflower's stalk. Cut the cauliflower into 8 wedges. Combine turmeric and pepper flakes. Slices are oiled and then sprinkled with a turmeric-turmeric powder mixture.
2. Grill covered over medium-high heat for 8–10 minutes on each side, or broil cauliflower at 4 inches from the heat source, until it is tender. If preferred, garnish with pomegranate seeds, more oil, and a squeeze of fresh lemon juice.

Nutrition Information[per serving]
Calories 58 | Fat 3.8g | Total Carbohydrate 5.9g | Sugars 1.8g | Protein 2.1g | Potassium 317mg | Sodium 32 mg
Storage a sealed container is used to store Grilled Cauliflower Wedges for up to 3 -4 days.
Reheat: just defrost at room temperature for a few hours

10.3 Garlic Mashed Cauliflower

Preparation: 10 minutes
Cooking time: 15 minutes
Servings :4
Ingredients

- white pepper -1/8 tsp. (1/2 g)
- coconut milk -3 tbsp. (45 ml)
- salt -1/2 tsp. (2 g)
- Garlic clove - 1
- Optional: Cracked black pepper and minced fresh chives
- fresh cauliflowers- 5 cups (500 g)
- reduced-fat mayonnaise -3 tbsp. (42 ml)

Preparation

1. Bring the garlic, cauliflower, and 1 inch of water to a boil in a large pot. Reduce the heat to low, cover, and cook the vegetables for 12 minutes or until soft. After draining the garlic and cauliflower, return them to the pan.
2. To achieve the appropriate consistency, mash the cauliflower combination. Add the milk, mayonnaise, salt, and pepper while stirring. Add some chives and cracked pepper, if preferred.

Nutrition Information[per serving]
Calories 88 | Fat 5.2g | Total Carbohydrate 9.2g | Sugars 4.2g | Protein 2.9g | Potassium 402mg | Sodium 77 mg
Storage a sealed container is used to store Garlic Mashed Cauliflower for up to 3 -4 days.
Reheat: just defrost at room temperature for a few hours

10.4 Broccoli Cauliflower Combo

Preparation: 10 minutes
Cooking time: 10 minutes
Servings :6
Ingredients

- pepper -1/8 tsp.(1/2 g)
- dried basil -1 tsp. (4 g)
- seasoned salt -1/2 tsp. (2 g)
- fresh broccoli florets -4 cups (450 g)
- Shallots, chopped -3
- reduced-sodium chicken broth or vegetable broth -1/2 cup (120 ml)
- fresh cauliflowers -2 cups (200 g)

Preparation

1. Combine all ingredients in a sizable cast-iron skillet or other sturdy pan. Vegetables should be crisp-tender after 6 to 8 minutes of cooking under cover at medium heat while being stirred occasionally.

Nutrition Information[per serving]
Calories 43 | Fat 0.4g | Total Carbohydrate 8.1g | Sugars 2.3g | Protein 3.5g | Potassium 393mg | Sodium 113 mg
Storage a sealed container is used to store Broccoli Cauliflower Combo for up to 3 -4 days.
Reheat: just defrost at room temperature for a few hours

10.5 Baked apples with cherries and almonds

Preparation: 10 minutes
Cooking time: 10 minutes
Servings :6
Ingredients

- ground cinnamon -1/2 tsp.(2 g)
- wheat germ -1 tbsp.(15 g)
- brown sugar -1 tbsp.(15 g)
- ground nutmeg -1/8 tsp. (1/2 g)
- small Golden Delicious apples -6
- dried cherries, coarsely chopped -1/3 cup

- apple juice -1/2 cup (120 ml)
- dark honey -2 tbsp.(30 g)
- water - 1/4 cup (60 ml)
- walnut oil or canola oil -2 tsp. (8 g)
- chopped almonds -3 tbsp.(45 g)

Preparation

1. Turn the oven to 350 degrees Fahrenheit (176 C).
2. In a small mixing basin, combine the nutmeg, cinnamon, brown sugar, wheat germ, almonds, and cherries. Set aside.
3. You can eat the apples with or without the peeling. It is preferable to use a vegetable peeler or a sharp knife to remove the peel from each apple in a circular motion, skipping every other row so that the rows of apple flesh and the rows of skin alternate. Start apple coring at the stem end, stopping about 3/4 of the way down.
4. Push the cherry mixture carefully into each apple hole after dividing it up evenly. Put the apples in a compact baking dish that can go straight into the oven, or a large, heavy frying pan that is just big enough to keep them upright. The pan calls for both water and apple juice. After you've brushed the apples with honey and oil, you should wrap the entire baking dish with aluminium foil. For best results, check the apples with a knife after 50-60 minutes of baking.
5. Once the apples have been plated, pour the pan juices over them. Serve warm or at room temperature.

Nutrition Information[per serving]

Calories 159|Fat 2.6g|Total Carbohydrate 31.9g| Sugars 1.8g|Protein 1.3g|Potassium 300 mg|Sodium 3 mg

Storage a sealed container is used to store Baked apples with cherries and almonds for up to 3 -4 days.

Reheat: just defrost at room temperature for a few hours

10.6 Brown rice pilaf

Preparation: 10 minutes
Cooking time: 10 minutes
Servings :6

Ingredients

- olive oil -1 tbsp. (15 ml)
- finely grated Swiss cheese -2 tbsp. (30 g)
- onion, chopped -1
- fresh mushrooms-2 cups (140 g)
- chopped fresh parsley -1/2 cup (30 g)
- asparagus tips, cut in 1-inch pieces -2 cups (268 g)
- brown rice -1 cup (190 g)
- ground nutmeg -1/8 tsp.(1/2 g)
- water -3 cups (720 ml)

Preparation

1. Over medium heat, warm the olive oil in a big pot. Rice should be added and sauteed until it turns golden brown.
2. Water, bouillon granules, onion, mushrooms, and nutmeg should all be added gradually. Mixture should be brought to a boil, then simmered, covered, for 30 minutes. To prevent the mixture from drying out, add water as needed.
3. Include the asparagus tips, cover, and simmer for an additional five minutes. Add the cheese, then stir. Add parsley as a garnish. Serve right away.

Nutrition Information[per serving]

Calories166| Fat 4g|Total Carbohydrate 28.9g|Sugars 1.8g|Protein 5.3g|Potassium 208mg|Sodium 15 mg

Storage a sealed container is used to store Brown rice pilaf for up to 3 -4 days.

Reheat: just defrost at room temperature for a few hours

10.7 Quinoa cakes

Preparation: 10 minutes
Cooking time: 50 minutes
Servings :14
Ingredients

- garlic -3 cloves
- finely chopped fresh parsley -2 tbsp. (8 g)
- Gruyere or Parmesan cheese, shredded -6 ounces (170 g)
- sweet potatoes -3
- ground black pepper -1/4 tsp. (1 g)
- olive oil -2 tbsp. (30 ml)
- salt -1 tsp.(4 g)
- nutmeg-1/4 tsp. (1 g)
- uncooked quinoa -1 cup (170 g)
- eggs -2

Preparation

1. The oven's temperature is 375 F. (190 C). placing the potatoes on a baking sheet that has been prepped. Potatoes should be baked for 45 minutes, or until extremely tender. Prepare the quinoa as directed on the package, then set it aside to cool.
2. Combine the cooked sweet potatoes, cooked quinoa, eggs, cheese, garlic, parsley, salt, pepper, and nutmeg in a sizable bowl.
3. In a big pot, warm 1 tablespoon of olive oil. To add to the pan, half of the quinoa mixture must be shaped into patties that are each 1/4 cup in size. The cakes should be baked till golden brown. Place the cooked patties in a single layer on a baking sheet. Rerun the process using the remaining oil and the quinoa mixture. To make sure cakes are thoroughly heated, bake them in the oven for 5 minutes.

Nutrition Information[per serving]
Calories 187 | Fat 8.6g | Total Carbohydrate 20g | Sugars 0.3g | Protein 7.8g | Potassium 208mg | Sodium 156 mg

Storage a sealed container is used to store Quinoa cakes for up to 3 -4 days.
Reheat: just defrost at room temperature for a few hours

10.8 Tangy green beans

Preparation: 10 minutes
Cooking time: 10 minutes
Servings :10
Ingredients

- pepper-1/4 tsp.(1 g)
- green beans -1 1/2 pounds (680 g)
- sweet red bell peppers- 1/3 cup (50 g)
- salt -1/4 tsp.(1 g)
- garlic powder -1/8 tsp (1/2 g)
- olive oil or canola oil -4 1/2 tsp. (16 ml)
- water-4 1/2 tsp. (16 ml)
- vinegar -1 1/2 tsp (6 ml)
- mustard-1 1/2 tsp (6 g)

Preparation

1. In a steamer basket over water, steam red peppers and beans until they are crisp-tender. In a small bowl, whisk together all the remaining ingredients. Transfer the beans to a bowl for serving. Mix the addition of the dressing.

Nutrition Information[per serving]
Calories 75 | Fat 2.4g | Total Carbohydrate 8.2g | Sugars 7g | Protein 5 g | Potassium 240mg | Sodium 137 mg
Storage a sealed container is used to store Tangy green beans for up to 3 -4 days.
Reheat: just defrost at room temperature for a few hours

10.9 Roasted green beans

Preparation: 10 minutes
Cooking time: 10 minutes
Servings :4

Ingredients

- garlic -1 tbsp. (15 g)
- dried basil -1 tsp (4 g)
- onion powder-1 tsp (4 g)
- dried oregano-1 tsp (4 g)
- green beans -2 cups (220 g)
- pepper-1/2 tsp (2 g)
- salt -1/2 tsp (2 g)
- olive oil -2 tsp.(8 ml)
- cherry tomatoes - 20

Preparation

1. A temperature of 400 degrees Fahrenheit (204 degrees Celsius) is recommended for baking. Lightly grease a baking sheet.
2. Add the pepper, salt, basil, green beans, oil, garlic, tomatoes, oregano, and onion powder to a medium bowl. Then, thoroughly combine the ingredients.
3. Before placing the green beans on the baking sheet, spread them out equally. After 13 minutes of roasting in the oven, stir once.

Nutrition Information[per serving]

Calories 52|Fat 2.8g|Total Carbohydrate 7.3g|Sugars 2.2g|Protein 1.7g|Potassium 246 mg|Sodium 297 mg

Storage a sealed container is used to store Roasted green beans for up to 3 -4 days.

Reheat: just defrost at room temperature for a few hours

10.10 Granola with raisins, apples and cinnamon

Preparation: 10 minutes
Cooking time: 10 minutes
Servings :12

Ingredients

- unsweetened applesauce-1/4 cup (61 g)
- honey -1/4 cup (84 g)
- slivered almonds -1/4 cup (27 g)
- golden raisins -1/2 cup (72 g)
- bran flakes -2 cups (60 g)
- ground cinnamon -1 tbsp. (7 g)
- dry old-fashioned oatmeal -2 cups (162 g)
- vanilla extract -1 tbsp. (13 g)
- dried apple pieces -3/4 cup (88 g)

Preparation

1. An oven temperature of 325 °F (162 C). Apply cooking spray sparingly to a baking sheet.
2. Roast the almonds on a baking sheet for approximately 10 minutes, stirring once or twice, until aromatic and toasted. Transfer to a platter to cool immediately. The oven temperature is 350 degrees Fahrenheit (176 degrees Celsius).
3. Combine the honey, applesauce, vanilla, and cinnamon in another bowl. Place aside.
4. Distribute the bran flakes and oatmeal into a sizable bowl. Stir vigorously to combine. With your hands, blend the honey mixture, then add it. Do not split the clusters.
5. Distribute the cereal mixture equally on a baking sheet. Place in the oven for 30 minutes, stirring occasionally, or until golden brown. Allow the meal to cool after removing it from the oven.
6. In a large mixing dish, combine the toasted almonds, dried apples, raisins, and cereal. Once cooling is complete, use an airtight container for storage.

Nutrition Information[per serving]
Calories 138|Fat 2.1g|Total Carbohydrate 28.7g|Sugars 13g |Protein 3.1g|Potassium 177mg|Sodium 51 mg

Storage a sealed container is used to store Granola with raisins, apples and cinnamon for up to 3 -4 days.

Reheat: just defrost at room temperature for a few hours

10.11 Savoury buckwheat pilaf with toasted spices

Preparation: 10 minutes
Cooking time: 10 minutes
Servings :6

Ingredients

- chopped fresh cilantro (coriander) -2 tbsp.(2 g)
- olive oil -1 tbsp. (15 ml)
- ground cardamom -1/4 tsp (1 g)
- cumin seed -1/2 tsp (2 g)
- garlic cloves -3
- salt -1/4 tsp (1 g)
- buckwheat groats -1 cup (120 g)
- onion -1
- tomato -1
- vegetable stock or broth -2 cups (480 ml)
- mustard seed-1/2 tsp (2 g)

Preparation

1. Over a low heat, melt the olive oil in a saucepan. After being added, the onion should be soft and transparent after 4 minutes of cooking. Add the garlic, mustard seed, cumin, cardamom, and buckwheat groats. The spices and garlic will start to smell delicious after three minutes of constant stirring, and the buckwheat will only just start to toast.

2. Pour the stock in with care. Bring to a boil, then reduce the heat to medium-low, cover the pan, and simmer for 10 minutes, or until the liquid is completely absorbed. Remove the saucepan from the heat, cover it, and let it rest for two minutes.

3. A tomato and salt are present. Transferring to a serving basin after adding the cilantro. Serve immediately.

Nutrition Information
Calories 114|Fat 3.6g |Total Carbohydrate 17.3g|Sugars 1.8g|Protein 4.7g|Potassium 249mg|Sodium 259 mg

Storage a sealed container is used to store Savory buckwheat pilaf with toasted spices for up to 3 -4 days.

Reheat: just defrost at room temperature for a few hours

10.12 Green beans with red pepper and garlic

Preparation: 10 minutes
Cooking time: 10 minutes
Servings :6

Ingredients

- chili paste or red pepper flakes -1/2 tsp (2g)
- olive oil -2 tsp (8 g)
- red bell pepper -1
- salt -1/4 tsp (1 g)
- green beans, -1 pound (450 g)
- garlic -1 clove
- freshly ground black pepper-1/4 tsp (1 g)
- sesame oil -1 tsp (4 g)

Preparation

1. Cut the beans into 2-inch-long pieces. Large kettle of water brought to a boil. After boiling the beans for 1 to 3 minutes, they should be bright green and crisp-tender. To halt the cooking process, immediately drain the beans and place them in a dish of ice water. Drain once more, after which remove.

2. Melt the olive oil in a large frying pan over medium heat. For about a minute, add the bell pepper and blend while

tossing. Continue to sauté for one more minute after adding the beans. Stir for a minute after adding the garlic and chile paste. Green beans with a vibrant flavour will be served. Salt and pepper should also be added, along with a dab of sesame oil. Serve right away.

Nutrition Information[per serving]
Calories 52 | Fat 2.5g | Total Carbohydrate 7.3g | Sugars 2.2g | Protein 1.7g | Potassium 199mg | Sodium 107 mg

Storage a sealed container is used to store Green beans with red pepper and garlic for up to 3 -4 days.

Reheat: just defrost at room temperature for a few hours

10.13 Peanut butter hummus

Preparation: 10 minutes
Cooking time: 10 minutes
Servings : 16

Ingredients

- vanilla extract -1 tsp (4 g)
- natural peanut butter -1/4 cup (45 g)
- powdered peanut butter -1/2 cup (60 g)
- water -1 cup (240 ml)
- brown sugar -2 tbsp. (30 g)
- garbanzo beans -2 cups (400 g)

Preparation

1. All the ingredients should be placed in a food processor. until smooth, process. Keep chilled for up to a week.

Nutrition Information[per serving]
Calories133 | Fat 3.8g | Total Carbohydrate 17.7g | Sugars 4.2g | Protein 7.4g | Potassium 208mg | Sodium 13 mg

Storage a sealed container is used to store Peanut butter hummus for up to 7 days.

Reheat: just defrost at room temperature for a few hours

11 FISH & SEAFOOD

11.1 Tasty Baked Fish

Preparation: 10 minutes
Cooking time: 10 minutes
Servings :4

Ingredients

- ground rosemary-1/2 tsp (2 g)
- black pepper-1/2 tsp (2 g)
- cod fillets -1 pound (450 g)
- olive oil -2 tbsp. (30 ml)
- ground cumin -1/2 tsp (2 g)

Preparation

2. Set the oven to 350° F (176C).
3. Fish fillets should be flattened and thoroughly coated in oil by turning them several times.
4. Fish should be spiced.
5. Put inside a baking dish.
6. Bake for about 20 to 25 minutes, or until fish flakes easily when tested with a fork.

Nutrition Information[per serving]

Calories 153|Fat 8.1 g|Total Carbohydrate 0.4g|Sugars 0g|Protein 20.2g|Potassium 9mg|Sodium 71 mg

Storage a sealed container is used to store Tasty Baked Fish for up to 7 days.

Reheat: just defrost at room temperature for a few hours

11.2 Creamy Shrimp and Broccoli Fettuccine

Preparation: 10 minutes
Cooking time: 10 minutes
Servings : 4

Ingredients

- cream cheese -10 ounces (283 g)
- garlic powder -1/2 tsp (2g)
- half & half creamer -1/4 cup (50 g)
- ground peppercorns -3/4 tsp (3g)
- red bell pepper -1/4 cup (40 g)
- broccoli florets -1-3/4 cup (160 g)
- garlic clove -1
- fettuccine, uncooked -4 ounces (113 g)
- frozen medium shrimp -3/4 pound (337 g)
- lemon juice -1/4 cup (60 ml)

Preparation

1. While cooking the pasta, leave out the salt.
2. In the final three minutes of cooking, add the broccoli. Drain. Stay warm.
3. In a sizable nonstick skillet over medium heat, sauté and toss shrimp and garlic for 2 to 3 minutes, or until shrimp are thoroughly cooked.
4. Add cream cheese, minced peppercorns, lemon juice, garlic powder, and half-and-half. For two minutes, cook and stir.
5. Combine the shrimp and noodles. Add some bell pepper flakes.

Nutrition Information[per serving]

Calories 446|Fat 27.1g|Total Carbohydrate 20.3g|Sugars 1.3g|Protein 30.4g|Potassium 247mg|Sodium 173 mg

Storage a sealed container is used to store Creamy Shrimp and Broccoli Fettuccine for up to 3-4 days.

Reheat: just defrost at room temperature for a few hours

11.3 Baked Trout

Preparation: 10 minutes
Cooking time: 10 minutes
Servings : 8

Ingredients

- salt-free lemon pepper -1 tsp (4 g)

- rainbow trout fillets -2 pounds (900 g)
- salt -1/2 tsp (2 g)
- paprika-1/2 tsp (2 g)
- cooking oil -1 tbsp. (15 ml)

Preparation

1. Preheat the oven to 350 degrees Fahrenheit (176 C).
2. Wash the fillets and pat them dry. Apply oil sparingly and then rub.
3. The fillets should be put skin-down on a sizable sheet pan.
4. In a small bowl, mix the ingredients. liberally sprinkle over the fillets.
5. Bake the salmon fillets for 10 to 15 minutes without the cover on, or until they are cooked.

Nutrition Information[per serving]

Calories 233 | Fat 11.8g | Total Carbohydrate 0g | Sugars 0g | Protein 27.4g | Potassium 3mg | Sodium 13 mg

Storage a sealed container is used to store Baked Trout for up to 7 days.

Reheat: just defrost at room temperature for a few hours

11.4 Shrimp Fried Rice

Preparation: 10 minutes
Cooking time: 10 minutes
Servings : 4

Ingredients

- fresh ginger root -1 tbsp. (15 g)
- white long-grain rice, cooked and cooled -4 cups (560 g)
- eggs, beaten -4
- Onion -3/4 cup (120 g)
- peanut oil -5 tbsp.(75 ml)
- black pepper -3/4 tsp (3 g)
- frozen peas and carrots -1 cup (80 g)
- salt -1/4 tsp (1 g)
- small pre-cooked, frozen shrimp -1/2 cup (64 g)
- scallions -3 tbsp. (45g)
- garlic clove -1

Preparation

1. Chop scallions and dice an onion. Garlic and ginger root are minced.
2. In a sizable nonstick skillet, heat 1 tablespoon of oil over medium-high heat.
3. Cook for about 2 minutes, or until onion is soft, before adding onion and 1/2 teaspoon black pepper.
4. Stir for approximately a minute after adding the scallions, ginger, and garlic.
5. When hot, add the shrimp and stir regularly.
6. Stir in the peas and carrots until cooked. Put the shrimp and veggie combination in a sizable bowl with a lid.
7. Add 2 tablespoons of oil and put the skillet back on the stove. Scramble the eggs in the skillet until done. Add the eggs, shrimp, and vegetables to a bowl.
8. Add 1 tablespoon of oil and bring skillet back to a simmer. 4 cups of cooked rice should be added, heated, and oil-coated.
9. Rice should be salted and peppered before being set aside in a skillet for about two minutes without stirring.
10. Add eggs, veggies, and shrimp to the rice after stirring. Serve warm.

Nutrition Information[per serving]

Calories 442 | Fat 22.1g | Total Carbohydrate 47.7g | Sugars 3.2g | Protein 14.3g | Potassium 240mg | Sodium 363 mg

Storage a sealed container is used to store Shrimp Fried Rice for up to 3-4 days.

Reheat: just defrost at room temperature for a few hours

11.5 Citrus Salmon

Preparation: 10 minutes
Cooking time: 15 minutes
Servings : 6

Ingredients

- butter -1 tbsp. (15 g)

- Dijon mustard-1 tbsp. (15 g)
- capers -1 tbsp. (10 g)
- cayenne pepper -2 dashes
- salmon filet -24 ounces (680 g)
- dried dill-1 tsp (4 g)
- olive oil -2 tbsp. (30 ml)
- garlic cloves -2
- lemon juice -1-1/2 tbsp. (22 ml)
- dried basil leaves -1 tsp (4 g)

Preparation

1. First, crush the garlic.
2. Combine all the ingredients in a small pot, excluding the fish. Turn the heat to low when it comes to a boil, and simmer for an additional five minutes.
3. Meanwhile, preheat the grill. Place the salmon skin-side down on a slightly larger-than-fish piece of aluminum foil. Fold up the edges so that the sauce stays with the grilled fish. There are fish and foil on the grill. Pour the sauce previously made over the fish.
4. Salmon should be grilled with a cover for 12 minutes. (Avoid rotating the salmon.) Cut up the salmon into six servings.

Nutrition Information[per serving]

Calories 551 |Fat 11.8g|Total Carbohydrate 22.3g|Sugars 0.1g|Protein 0.3g|Potassium 20mg|Sodium 139 mg

Storage a sealed container is used to store Peanut butter hummus for up to 3-5 days.

Reheat: just defrost at room temperature for a few hours

11.6 Super Tuesday Shrimp

Preparation: 10 minutes

Cooking time: 10 minutes

Servings : 4

Ingredients

- pasta, uncooked -4 ounces (113 g)
- feta cheese -1/4 cup (35 g)
- frozen pea pods, -8 ounces (226 g)

- olive oil -1 tbsp. (15 ml)
- onion -2 tbsp. (30 g)
- medium shrimp, uncooked -12 ounces (340 g)
- garlic cloves -2
- sun dried tomatoes in oil -1/4 cup (25 g)

Preparation

1. Without adding salt, prepare pasta as directed on the package. Drain, then set apart.
2. Onion and garlic are minced. Devein and shell the shrimp.
3. Garlic and onion should be lightly browned in oil.
4. Add shrimp, pea pods, and sun-dried tomatoes.
5. Cook shrimp until they change colour (but pea pods remain crunchy).
6. Combine pasta and shrimp.
7. Serve the dish with feta cheese on top.

Nutrition Information[per serving]

Calories 253|Fat 7.5g |Total Carbohydrate 22.2g|Sugars 3.5g|Protein 25g|Potassium 193mg|Sodium 133 mg

Storage a sealed container is used to store Super Tuesday Shrimp for up to 7 days.

Reheat: just defrost at room temperature for a few hours

11.7 Grilled Mexican Swordfish Fillets

Preparation: 10 minutes

Cooking time: 10 minutes

Servings: 6

Ingredients

- fresh cilantro-1/4 tsp. (1 g)
- Serrano chile -1
- vegetable oil- 1 tbsp. (15 ml)
- fresh lime juice -1/4 cup (60 ml)
- onion -1/4 cup (40 g)
- swordfish fillets -1-1/2 pounds (680 g)
- sugar -1 tbsp. (15 g)

- lime -1
- salt -1/4 tsp. (1 g)
- garlic cloves -2

Preparation

1. Chop an onion. Chipotle should be seeded and chopped finely.
2. Put the fish in a baking dish that is oven-safe.
3. Blend or process the following ingredients until smooth: cilantro, onion, sugar, chile, lime juice, oil, and 1/4 teaspoon salt.
4. Then, turn the fish to coat with the combination of cilantro. Marinate for at least 30 minutes in the refrigerator, turning once halfway through.
5. Prepare and heat a grill for charcoal or gas.
6. Fish should be grilled for about 5 minutes total, or until it flakes easily with a fork.
7. Lime should be wedged. Serve fish with lime wedges as a garnish.

Nutrition Information

Calories 149|Fat 6.2g |Total Carbohydrate 3g|Sugars 2.3g|Protein 19.3g|Potassium 296mg|Sodium 183 mg

Storage a sealed container is used to store Grilled Mexican Swordfish Fillets for up to 7 days.

Reheat: just defrost at room temperature for a few hours

11.8 Easy Shrimp in Garlic Sauce

Preparation: 10 minutes
Cooking time: 10 minutes
Servings : 4

Ingredients

- white wine-1/4 cup (25 ml)
- half & half creamer -1/4 cup (60 g)
- black pepper -1/8 tsp (1/2 g)
- fresh basil -2 tbsp. (12 g)
- whipped cream cheese -1/2 cup

- bowtie pasta, uncooked -8 ounces (226 g)
- raw shrimp -1 pound (450 g)
- onion -1/4 cup (60 g)
- unsalted butter -3 tbsp.(45 g)
- garlic cloves -3

Preparation

1. Devein and shell the shrimp.
2. Bring 3 quarts of water to a boil in a large pot. Add 3 cups of dried bowtie pasta and cook for 12 minutes before draining.
3. While the pasta is boiling, mince the garlic and onion. Melt the butter in a pan over medium heat. One minute of cooking the onion and garlic. When the shrimp becomes orange, add it and boil for 1 to 2 minutes (do not overcook).
4. Take the shrimp out of the pan and set it aside. Low-heat setting. To prepare a sauce, add cream cheese to the skillet along with the onion, garlic, and butter.
5. Stir in the half-and-half creamer. Wine should be added and thoroughly mixed. Stirred cooked shrimp back into the sauce to coat.
6. Pasta should be drained, divided among 4 plates, and topped with garlic-shrimp sauce. Black pepper and 1/2 tablespoon freshly chopped basil are used as seasonings.

Nutrition Information[per serving]

Calories 458|Fat 12.1g|Total Carbohydrate 47.7g|Sugars 2.2g|Protein 37.4g|Potassium 281mg|Sodium 143 mg

Storage a sealed container is used to store Easy Shrimp in Garlic Sauce for up to 7 days.

Reheat: just defrost at room temperature for a few hours

11.9 Grilled Salmon with Herb Crust

Preparation: 10 minutes
Cooking time: 10 minutes
Servings : 4

Ingredients

- garlic clove – 1
- green onion -1/4 cup (25 g)
- lemon juice -1 tbsp. (15 ml)
- salt -1/4 tsp (1 g)
- cilantro -1/3 cup (3 g)
- black pepper-1/4 tsp (1 g)
- olive oil-1 tbsp. (15 ml)
- skinless salmon fillets -12 ounces (340 g)
- oregano -1/2 cup (24 g)

Preparation

1. Heat the grill or oven to 400 degrees Fahrenheit (204 C).
2. Ensure that each salmon fillet has an aluminum foil cooking pocket (if using frozen salmon, make sure it has fully thawed).
3. To a fine consistency, chop the garlic, green onions, oregano, and cilantro. In a food processor, pepper, salt, olive oil, and lemon juice should be mixed.
4. Drizzle the herb mixture generously over the salmon fillets.
5. Fillet-containing foil pockets must be sealed.
6. When grilling, place foil pockets on a baking sheet or grill plate.
7. Bake for 30 minutes, or, depending on the thickness, grill for 6 to 8 minutes.

Nutrition Information[per serving]

Calories 213|Fat 13.8g|Total Carbohydrate 6.7g|Sugars 0.2g |Protein17.4g|Potassium 184mg|Sodium 53 mg

Storage a sealed container is used to store Grilled Salmon with Herb Crust for up to 7 days.

Reheat: just defrost at room temperature for a few hours

11.10 Lively Lime Shrimp

Preparation: 10 minutes
Cooking time: 10 minutes
Servings : 4

Ingredients

- lime juice -1/4 cup (60 ml)
- cucumber -1
- shrimp -32
- olive oil -2 tbsp. (30 ml)
- salt -1/8 tsp (1/2 g)
- jalapeno chili -1 tbsp. (6 g)
- fresh cilantro -2 tbsp. (6g)
- red bell pepper -3 tbsp .(45 g)
- green onion -1
-
- garlic clove -1

Preparation

1. Chop the cilantro and onion. mince the bell pepper, garlic, and chilli. Slice the cucumbers thinly.
2. Devein and peel the shrimp.
3. To make the dressing, mix the lime juice, oil, garlic, salt, cilantro, and jalapeno in a medium bowl.
4. To marinate the shrimp, combine 2 tablespoons of the dressing with a medium bowl of shrimp. Keep any dressing that is left over. Refrigeration under cover for 30 minutes.
5. Bring up the broiler. The shrimp should be taken out of the marinade and broiled for one and a half minutes on each side, or until opaque, at a distance of three inches from the heat source.
6. Take shrimp out of the broiler and combine them immediately away with the conserved dressing and red bell pepper. Cool till room temperature.
7. Arrange the shrimp atop cucumber slices and serve.

Nutrition Information[per serving]
Calories 155 | Fat 8.1 g | Total Carbohydrate
10.9g | Sugars 5.9g | Protein 11.6g | Potassium
376mg | Sodium 183 mg

Storage a sealed container is used to store Lively Lime Shrimp for up to 7 days.

Reheat: just defrost at room temperature for a few hours

11.11 Linguine with Garlic and Shrimp

Preparation: 10 minutes

Cooking time: 15 minutes

Servings : 6

Ingredients

- lemon juice -1 tbsp. (15 ml)
- black pepper -1/4 tsp. (1g)
- linguine, uncooked -12 ounces (340 g)
- garlic, whole -2 heads
- water -2-1/2 quarts (2L)
- raw shrimp -3/4 pound (338 g)
- olive oil -2 tbsp. (30 ml)
- flat-leaf parsley -1 cup (60 g)

Preparation

1. Clean and peel shrimp. Trim the parsley.
2. The water in a large saucepan is boiling. The pasta should be cooked for 10 minutes or until al dente.
3. While the pasta is cooking, separate the garlic cloves, leaving the peel intact. Toast the cloves in a frying skillet over medium heat, turning them constantly. When garlic turns brown and becomes touchable, it is ready for consumption. Skin will be straightforward to remove. Remove the garlic from the pan and remove its skin.
4. Garlic that has been peeled is added to the hot oil in the frying pan. until golden, sauté the garlic. (You can chop cloves in half or leave them whole.)
5. Cook the shrimp for 2 minutes, stirring periodically, until pink. Add parsley.

6. Drain the pasta and reserve 1 cup of the cooking liquid. Add pasta to the garlic and shrimp in the pan. Mix all ingredients together, then whisk in the liquid from the reserved cup.
7. Add black pepper and lemon juice. Stir, then plate.

Nutrition Information[per serving]
Calories 277 | Fat 8g | Total Carbohydrate
33g | Sugars 0.2g | Protein 19.4g | Potassium 264
mg | Sodium 163 mg

Storage a sealed container is used to store Linguine with Garlic and Shrimp for up to 7 days.

Reheat: just defrost at room temperature for a few hours

11.12 Shrimp-Stuffed Deviled Eggs

Preparation: 10 minutes

Cooking time: 10 minutes

Servings : 6

Ingredients

- eggs, hard boiled -6
- mayonnaise -1-1/2 tbsp. (21 g)
- mustard -1/2 tsp (2 g)
- cooked shrimp -1/2 cup (40 g)
- lemon juice-1/2 tsp (2 ml)
- black pepper-1/4 tsp (1 g)

Preparation

1. Cut cooked eggs lengthwise in half. Remove yolks with care, then put them in a basin.
2. Add egg yolks, mustard, mayonnaise, lemon juice, and pepper to shrimp that has been finely chopped. Mix all items together thoroughly.
3. Fill egg white halves with a mixture of shrimp and yolks.

Nutrition Information[per serving]
Calories 91 | Fat 6g | Total Carbohydrate
1.3g | Sugars 0.2g | Protein 8g | Potassium
83mg | Sodium 103 mg

Storage a sealed container is used to store Shrimp-Stuffed Deviled Eggs for up to 7 days.

Reheat: just defrost at room temperature for a few hours

11.13 Steamed Whole Fish

Preparation: 10 minutes

Cooking time: 10 minutes

Servings : 8

Ingredients

- Sea Bass or Tilapia Fish of choice -1.5 lbs – (680 grams)
- Sesame oil/Vegetable oil -2 tbsp. (30 ml)
- Ginger sliced thinly -¼ cup
- Water -¼ cup (60 ml)
- Soy Sauce - 1 tbsp. (15 ml)
- Scallions thinly sliced and long -2

Preparation

1. Clean the fish well, take off the scales and fins, and clean the insides to get rid of any necessary residue.
2. Place half of the ginger and scallions inside the fish after thinly slicing them. Keep the remainder for future use.
3. Set up your steaming apparatus and add 1-2 inches of water to a deep wok or pan. Carefully set a plate with the fish on it on top of the steam rack. the water will be boiled.
4. Put a lid on the wok. The fish should be steam-cooked for 8 to 12 minutes, or until the flesh is opaque and flakes easily. Add the remaining ginger and scallions as a garnish.
5. After the fish has finished steaming, warm the sesame oil and low-sodium soy sauce in a separate skillet and drizzle it over the prepared fish. Serve right away!

Nutrition Information[per serving]

Calories 133|Fat 3.8g|Total Carbohydrate 17.7g|Sugars 4.2g |Protein7.4g|Potassium 208mg|Sodium 13 mg

Storage a sealed container is used to store Steamed Whole Fish for up to 7 days.

Reheat: just defrost at room temperature for a few hours

11.14 Fish Cakes

Preparation: 10 minutes

Cooking time: 10 minutes

Servings : 16

Ingredients

- bread crumbs - 3 cups (324 g)
- butter for cooking -1/4 cup (56 g)
- Cod -2 lbs (1 kg)
- pepper ¼ tsp (1 ml)
- small onions -2

Preparation

1. Fish should be cut into pieces and combined with onions, breadcrumbs, and pepper in a basin.
2. Use a food processor or a meat grinder to process the mixture.
3. Make patties out of the pulverised mixture; if you use 2 pounds of fish and make the patties 3 inches in diameter and 12 inch thick, you should get about 18 fish cakes.
4. For five minutes on each side, fry the patties in butter.

Nutrition Information[per serving]

Calories 150|Fat 3.8g |Total Carbohydrate 13.7g|Sugars 1.2g|Protein 14g|Potassium 171mg|Sodium 190 mg

Storage a sealed container is used to store Fish Cakes for up to 7 days.

Reheat: just defrost at room temperature for a few hours

11.15 Shrimp and Apple Stir Fry

Preparation: 10 minutes

Cooking time: 10 minutes

Servings : 4

Ingredients

- Apple -3/4

- Sweet red pepper -2
- Celery stalks, -2
- Vegetable oil -2 tbsp. (30 mL)
- Headless shrimp with shells -1/2 lb (227 g)

Marinade

- Cornstarch -1 tsp (5 mL)
- Low sodium soy sauce -1/2 tsp (2.5 mL)
- Dash of White pepper

Sauce

- Low sodium soy sauce -1/2 tsp (2.5 mL)
- Sugar -1 tsp (5 mL)
- Cornstarch -1 tsp (5 mL)
- Cold water -2 tbsp (30 mL)

Preparation

1. Devein and shell the shrimp. The shrimp should be marinated for 30 minutes using the ingredients above.
2. In a small bowl, combine the ingredients for the sauce. Mix completely before pausing.
3. In a nonstick skillet, heat approximately 1 tablespoon of oil. The shrimp should be removed from the pan once they have been stir-fried until they turn pink.
4. In a nonstick skillet, heat approximately 1 tablespoon of oil. When the celery is almost fully cooked, add the apple and red pepper immediately. Once the sauce begins to thicken, add the shrimp and stir continuously. ready to assist.

Nutrition Information[per serving]

Calories 121 | Fat 8.6g | Total Carbohydrate 11.7g | Sugars 6.6g | Protein 1g | Potassium 97mg | Sodium 77 mg

Storage a sealed container is used to store Shrimp and Apple Stir Fry for up to 7 days.

Reheat: just defrost at room temperature for a few hours

11.16 Maple Broiled Salmon

Preparation: 10 minutes

Cooking time: 10 minutes

Servings : 4

Ingredients

- maple syrup -3 tbsp. (45 ml)
- fresh cilantro -2 tbsp. (6 g)
- lemon juice (or juice of 1 lemon) -3 tbsp. (45 ml)
- low sodium soy sauce -1 tbsp. (15 ml)
- green onion, chopped -1 tbsp. (15 g)
- salmon fillets -1 lb. (450 g)
- garlic cloves -2

Preparation

1. Combine everything else, excluding salmon.
2. Place salmon fillets on a dish and cover with marinade. Allow to sit for at least two hours.
3. Heat the broiler. Take the salmon out of the marinade. Cook each side for 4 to 8 minutes. If the flesh splits readily when prodded with a fork, the food has been cooked sufficiently.
4. Whether hot or cold, garnish with a lemon wedge.

Nutrition Information[per serving]

Calories 197 | Fat 7.1g | Total Carbohydrate 11.7g | Sugars 9.3g | Protein 22.4g | Potassium 208mg | Sodium 204 mg

Storage a sealed container is used to store Maple Broiled Salmon for up to 7 days.

Reheat: just defrost at room temperature for a few hours

12 POULTRY RECIPES

12.1 Chicken and Rice Casserole

Preparation: 10 minutes
Cooking time: 30 minutes
Servings : 6

Ingredients

- cooked white rice -3 cups (555 g)
- bell pepper -1 cup (149 g)
- black pepper -1/4 tsp (1 g)
- Worcestershire sauce -1 tbsp. (15 ml)
- cubed chicken, cooked -2 cups (280 g)
- Butter -2 tbsp. (30 g)
- reduced-sodium chicken broth -1 cup (240 ml)
- all-purpose flour -1/3 cup (42 g)
- onion -1/2 cup
- coconut milk -1 cup (240 ml)
- Mrs. Dash® herb seasoning blend -1 tbsp. (15 g)
- olive oil -2 tbsp. (30 ml)
- mushrooms -1 cup (70 g)

Preparation

1. 350 degrees Fahrenheit oven temperature (176 C). A 1-1/2 quart baking dish should be sprayed with nonstick cooking spray.
2. Finely chop the bell pepper and onion.
3. A large saucepan is used to gradually heat butter and olive oil.
4. After the butter has melted, mix in the pepper and flour. Cook the ingredients while stirring frequently until it is boiling and smooth. Eliminate the heat.
5. Stir in the chicken broth, milk, and Worcestershire sauce. Bring to a boil while continuously stirring. Stir while boiling for one minute.

6. Chicken, cooked rice, mushrooms, bell pepper, onion, and Mrs. Dash herb seasoning should all be stirred in.
7. Put into the baking pan. For 30 minutes, bake with a cover. After 20 minutes, remove the top and continue to cook.

Nutrition Information[per serving]
Calories 547 | Fat 11.1g | Total   Carbohydrate 84.7g | Sugars   4.3g | Protein   23.4g | Potassium 387mg | Sodium 204 mg

Storage a sealed container is used to store Chicken and Rice Casserole for up to 3-5 days.

Reheat: just defrost at room temperature for a few hours

12.2 Marinade for Grilled Chicken

Preparation: 10 minutes
Cooking time: 10 minutes
Servings : 8

Ingredients

- dried oregano -1/2 tsp (2 g)
- white distilled vinegar -1/2 cup (120 ml)
- canola oil -1/2 cup (120 ml)
- black pepper -1/4 tsp (1g)
- garlic powder-1/4 tsp (1g)

Preparation

1. In a small bowl, mix the marinade ingredients.
2. Pour over the chicken pieces of your choice, then marinate for one to four hours in the refrigerator.

Nutrition Information[per serving]
Calories 121 | Fat 13.1g | Total Carbohydrate 0.2g | Sugars 0g | Protein 0g | Potassium 2mg | Sodium 0 mg

Storage a sealed container is used to store Marinade for Grilled Chicken for up to 7 days.

Reheat: just defrost at room temperature for a few hours

12.3 Quick and Easy Chicken Stir-Fry

Preparation: 10 minutes
Cooking time: 10 minutes
Servings : 4
Ingredients

- canola oil -3 tbsp. (45 ml)
- broccoli slaw -10 ounce (283 g)
- cooked chicken breast -8 ounces (226 g)
- water-1/3 cup (80 ml)
- hoisin sauce -1/3 cup (11 g)

Preparation
1. Tear up the cooked chicken breast.
2. In a large pan, heat 1 tablespoon of the oil before adding the broccoli slaw and simmering for 5 minutes.
3. Add the remaining 2 tablespoons of oil, along with the water and hoisin sauce, to the wok. Combine; mash.
4. Add shredded chicken to the wok. In a bowl, mix the chicken and broccoli slaw.
5. You can add rice or rice noodles if you'd like.

Nutrition Information[per serving]
Calories 229 | Fat 12.9g | Total Carbohydrate 14.7g | Sugars 7g | Protein 14.7g | Potassium 460 mg | Sodium 204 mg

Storage a sealed container is used to store Quick and Easy Chicken Stir-Fry for up to 3-5 days.

Reheat: just defrost at room temperature for a few hours

12.4 Zesty Chicken

Preparation: 10 minutes
Cooking time: 10 minutes
Servings: 2
Ingredients

- green onion - 1/4 cup (25 g)
- paprika-1/4 tsp (1 g)
- olive oil-2 tbsp. (30 ml)
- balsamic vinegar -2 tbsp. (30 ml)
- black pepper -1/4 tsp (1 g)
- garlic powder -1/2 tsp (2 g)
- skinless, boneless chicken breast -8 ounces (226 g)
- fresh oregano -1 tsp (4 g)

Preparation
1. Combine the olive oil and balsamic vinegar in a measuring cup.
2. Add green onion, chopped, to the spices and herbs. whisking to combine.
3. Divide the bird in half. The marinade for the chicken should be placed in a leak-proof bowl or plastic storage bag. For 30 to 24 hours, marinate food in the refrigerator.
4. Take out the marinade from the chicken. For a few minutes on each side, completely cook in a nonstick or coated skillet at medium heat. The chicken breast's internal temperature need to be 170° F (as determined by a thermometer) (76 C).

Nutrition Information[per serving]
Calories 275 | Fat 17.1g | Total Carbohydrate 2.4g | Sugars 0.6g | Protein 25.4g | Potassium 75mg | Sodium 44 mg

Storage a sealed container is used to store Zesty Chicken for up to 3-5 days.

Reheat: just defrost at room temperature for a few hours

12.5 Lemon Oregano Chicken

Preparation: 10 minutes
Cooking time: 10 minutes
Servings : 8

Ingredients

- Oregano -1 tsp (4 g)
- Red Pepper Flakes - 1/4 tsp (1 g)
- Garlic Cloves -1
- Lemon, small -1
- Olive Oil -2 tbsp. (30 ml)
- Chicken breasts, boneless and skinless - 4
- Unsalted butter 2 tbsp. (30 g)
- Ground Black Peppercorns-1 tsp (4 g)

Preparation

1. Butterfly or carefully cut the chicken breasts in half. Garlic is minced, then placed aside. Lemons should be juiced and the juice left aside. Lemon juiced was cut into wheels.
2. Combine everything in a sizable mixing dish or freezer bag, leaving out the butter. Put this in the fridge and let it sit there for approximately an hour. timer for one hour.
3. A big pan should be heated to medium-high after adding 1 tablespoon of butter. To check whether the pan is hot enough, carefully add 1 piece of chicken there with tongs. Next, add three additional pieces of chicken and a few lemon wheels, then cook on each side for one to two minutes or until well-browned.
4. Repeat the previous process with the remaining 1 tbsp of butter and the remaining 4 pieces of chicken.
5. Remove the chicken from the skillet and set aside for 5 minutes before slicing and serving. Set a 5-minute timer.

Nutrition Information[per serving]

Calories 193|Fat   11.1g|Total Carbohydrate 3.3g|Sugars 0.3g |Protein20.4g|Potassium 187mg|Sodium 104 mg

Storage a sealed container is used to store Lemon Oregano Chicken for up to 7 days.

Reheat: just defrost at room temperature for a few hours

12.6 Roasted Rosemary Chicken and Vegetables

Preparation: 10 minutes
Cooking time: 10 minutes
Servings : 4

Ingredients

- ground pepper -1/4 tsp (1 g)
- red onion -1/2 large
- dried rosemary -1 tbsp. (4 g)
- chicken breasts, bone-in -4
- Carrots -1
- garlic cloves -8
- Zucchini -2
- bell pepper -1/2
- olive oil -1 tbsp. (15 ml)

Preparation

1. 375 degrees Fahrenheit (190 C) should be the oven's preheating temperature.
2. Slice the carrot and bell pepper 1/4" thick, the zucchini 1/2" thick, the onion into 1/2" slices, and crush the garlic cloves.
3. In a 13" x 9" roasting pan, mix the oil, zucchini, carrot, bell pepper, onion, and garlic. Add 1/2 teaspoon of black pepper to the mixture and toss to coat. For about 10 minutes, roast the vegetables until thoroughly cooked.
4. Remove the chicken breasts' skin and season the meat with cracked black pepper and rosemary while the vegetables are roasting. Once the skin has been replaced, season the chicken as desired with more pepper and rosemary.
5. Place the chicken, skin-side up, on top of the veggies in the roasting pan after

removing it from the oven. Return to the oven and roast the chicken and vegetables until they are done (about 35 minutes).

Nutrition Information[per serving]
Calories 177|Fat 7.4g |Total Carbohydrate 5.1g|Sugars 2g |Protein22.2g|Potassium 375mg|Sodium 74 mg
Storage a sealed container is used to store Roasted Rosemary Chicken and Vegetables for up to 7 days.
Reheat: just defrost at room temperature for a few hours

12.7 Honey Garlic Chicken

Preparation: 10 minutes
Cooking time: 10 minutes
Servings : 8
Ingredients
- black pepper -1/2 tsp (2 g)
- olive oil -1 tbsp. (15 ml)
- roasting chicken -4 pound (1814 g)
- garlic powder -1 tsp (4 g)
- honey -1/2 cup (170 g)

Preparation
1. Warm the oven to 350 degrees F (176 C).
2. Use olive oil to grease a baking pan.
3. Carefully arrange the pieces of chicken in the pan without touching. Apply seasonings and honey to the chicken.
4. Bake for about an hour, or until both sides are browned. Cooking involves one rotation.

Nutrition Information[per serving]
Calories 512|Fat 17.1g|Total Carbohydrate 17g|Sugars 9.3g |Protein 67.4g|Potassium 208mg|Sodium 196 mg
Storage a sealed container is used to store Honey Garlic Chicken for up to 7 days.
Reheat: just defrost at room temperature for a few hours

12.8 Crunchy Lemon-Herbed Chicken

Preparation: 10 minutes
Cooking time: 10 minutes
Servings : 4
Ingredients
- fresh thyme, chopped-1 tbsp. (2.5 g)
- lemon juice, plus zest of 1 lemon -¼ cup (60 ml)
- fresh oregano, chopped -1 tbsp. (4.5 g)
- panko bread crumbs -½ cup (54 g)
- water -3 tbsp. (45 ml)
- fresh basil, chopped-1 tbsp. (5.5 g)
- egg yolk -1
- unsalted butter, chilled -4 tbsp.(60 g)
- chicken tenders -6 2-ounce (340 g)

Preparation
1. 2 tablespoons of butter should be heated to a low temperature.
2. Add half the herbs and the zest of 1 lemon to the bread crumbs; reserve the other half for the lemon sauce.
3. Egg yolk and 1 tablespoon water are beaten.
4. Using the tiny groove side of the mallet, pound the chicken tenders between two sheets of plastic wrap until they are thin but not ripped.
5. After coating the chicken with herbed bread crumbs, it should be smeared with an egg wash mixture. Separate the two.
6. Set the temperature of 2 tablespoons of butter to medium.
7. A sauté pan containing breaded chicken
8. Cook the chicken for a total of two to three minutes.
9. The chicken should be taken out and given a baking sheet to rest on. The same pan should be heated to a simmer before adding the additional herbs and lemon juice.

10. Remove the sauce from the heat and rapidly stir in the remaining 2 Tablespoons of butter.
11. Cut the chicken into pieces.
12. Arrange the chicken slices on a dish, top with sauce, and add any garnishes you choose..

Nutrition Information[per serving]

Calories 339 | Fat 20g | Total Carbohydrate 11.7g | Sugars 1.3g | Protein27.4g | Potassium 287mg | Sodium 260 mg

Storage a sealed container is used to store Crunchy Lemon-Herbed Chicken for up to 7 days.

Reheat: just defrost at room temperature for a few hours

12.9 Rosemary Chicken

Preparation: 10 minutes

Cooking time: 10 minutes

Servings : 4

Ingredients

- crushed, dried rosemary -2 tsp (8 g)
- white wine -1/2 cup (60 g)
- Worcestershire sauce -1 tsp (4 g)
- oil -1/4 cup (60 ml)
- brown sugar -1/3 cup
- lime juice-1/4 cup (60 ml)
- broiler-fryer chicken, cut into quarters or split in half -1

Preparation

1. To make the marinade, place all the ingredients—aside from the chicken—in a small basin.
2. Place the chicken in the marinade and turn it to coat it completely. Cover and chill for at least 4 hours, rotating the meal as necessary. When you take the chicken from the marinade, reserve some for basting.
3. Place the chicken in the broiler pan skin-side down, approximately 7 to 9 inches from the heat source. Broil the chicken for 20 minutes, basting it occasionally with the marinade. After the chicken has been turned over, the chicken should be fork-tender after an additional 15 minutes of broiling.
4. Throw away any leftover marinade.

Nutrition Information[per serving]

Calories 266 | Fat 15.1g | Total Carbohydrate 12.7g | Sugars 12g | Protein 17.4g | Potassium 213mg | Sodium 81 mg

Storage a sealed container is used to store Rosemary Chicken for up to 7 days.

Reheat: just defrost at room temperature for a few hours

12.10 Dijon Chicken

Preparation: 10 minutes

Cooking time: 30 minutes

Servings : 4

Ingredients

- curry powder-1 tsp (4 g)
- Honey -3 tbsp. (45 g)
- Dijon mustard -1/4 cup
- chicken breasts -4 boneless
- lemon Juice -1 tsp (4 ml)

Preparation

1. Set the oven to 350 degrees Fahrenheit (176 C).
2. Place the chicken in the ovenproof dish.
3. In a bowl, combine the remaining ingredients.
4. Apply sauce on both sides of the chicken.
5. Bake the chicken for 30 minutes until the internal temperature reaches 165°F (76°C).

Nutrition Information[per serving]

Calories 338 | Fat 11.1g | Total Carbohydrate 14.7g | Sugars 13g | Protein 43g | Potassium 208mg | Sodium 204 mg

Storage a sealed container is used to store Dijon Chicken for up to 7 days.

Reheat: just defrost at room temperature for a few hours

12.11 Herb-Roasted Chicken Breasts

Preparation: 10 minutes

Cooking time: 30 minutes

Servings : 4

Ingredients

- ground black pepper -1 tsp (4 g)
- olive oil -¼ cup (60 ml)
- garlic cloves -1
- onion -1 medium
- Mrs. Dash® Garlic and Herb Seasoning Blend -2 tbsp.(30 g)
- boneless, skinless chicken breasts -1 pound (450 g)

Preparation

1. Add minced garlic and onion to a bowl. Pepper, Mrs. Dash Seasoning, and olive oil should be included.
2. The marinated chicken breasts should be added, covered, and refrigerated for at least 4 hours or overnight.

Baking:

1. Preheat the oven to 350° Fahrenheit (176 C).
2. A baking sheet with foil should be used to hold the marinated chicken breasts.
3. Brush the remaining marinade on the chicken after 20 minutes of baking at 350°F.
4. Broil for an additional five minutes to brown.

Nutrition Information[per serving]

Calories 337 | Fat   21.1g | Total Carbohydrate 3.2g | Sugars   1.3g | Protein33.4g | Potassium 325mg | Sodium 99 mg

Storage a sealed container is used to store Herb-Roasted Chicken Breasts for up to 7 days.

Reheat: just defrost at room temperature for a few hours

12.12 Moroccan Chicken

Preparation: 10 minutes

Cooking time: 40 minutes

Servings : 4

Ingredients

- lemon zest -½ tsp (2 g)
- black pepper-¼ tsp (1 g)
- ground cumin-½ tsp (2 g)
- paprika -1 tsp (4 g)
- sesame oil -1 tsp (4 ml)
- onion powder -¼ tsp (1 g)
- lemon juice - 2 tbsp. (30 ml)
- nutmeg-¼ tsp (1 g)
- cinnamon-¼ tsp (1 g)
- chicken breasts or thighs—bone in, no skin -6
- garlic—crushed -3 cloves
- Honey -1⁄3 cup (113 g)
- cayenne pepper½ tsp (2 g)

Preparation

1. All ingredients should be combined except chicken , followed by the chicken.
2. Refrigerate for 1 to 24 hours, turning occasionally.
3. A baking sheet should be foil-lined. Chicken should be placed bone-down on foil. Add the extra marinade with a spoon.
4. Bake at 400°F (204 C) for 30 to 40 minutes, or until well done.

Nutrition Information[per serving]

Calories 346 | Fat   11.8g | Total Carbohydrate 16.3g | Sugars   15.7g | Protein 42.4g | Potassium 208mg | Sodium 104 mg

Storage a sealed container is used to store Moroccan Chicken for up to 7 days.

Reheat: just defrost at room temperature for a few hours

12.13 Lemon Curry Chicken Salad

Preparation: 10 minutes
Cooking time: 00 minutes
Servings : 4

Ingredients

- frozen lemonade concentrate, thawed - 1/4 cup (60 ml)
- grapes, halved -1 1/2 cups (138 g)
- vegetable oil -1/4 cup (60 ml)
- chicken, cooked and diced -1 1/2 cups (210 g)
- ground ginger -1/4 tsp (1 g)
- curry powder-1/4 tsp (1 g)
- celery, sliced -1/2 cup (50 g)
- garlic powder -1/8 tsp (1/2 g)

Preparation

1. Mix the oil, lemonade concentrate, and spices in a sizable basin.
2. Combine the remaining ingredients, then gently toss.
3. For at least 1 hour, chill.

Nutrition Information[per serving]

Calories 259|Fat 15.4g|Total Carbohydrate 15.7g|Sugars 5.8g|Protein 15.4g|Potassium 214mg|Sodium 45 mg

Storage a sealed container is used to store Lemon Curry Chicken Salad for up to 7 days.

Reheat: just defrost at room temperature for a few hours

12.14 Chicken Tikka

Preparation: 10 minutes
Cooking time: 20 minutes
Servings : 4

Ingredients

- Curry paste -1 tbsp. (15 g)
- Coconut yogurt - 3 tbsp. (45 g)
- Lemon juice -1 tsp (4 ml)
- Chicken breasts (boneless, skinless) -2

Preparation

1. Curry paste and coconut yoghurt should be combined.
2. the yogurt-curry mixture, lemon juice, and chicken to a bowl. Allow the flavours to meld by letting it sit for an hour or even overnight.
3. heat up the grill and cook the chicken. 20 minutes should pass before the flesh becomes juicy. Serve it with lettuce shreds or in a tortilla wrap as a snack food. Serve it with boiling rice for the main course.

Nutrition Information[per serving]

Calories 196|Fat 8.1g |Total Carbohydrate 11.7g|Sugars 1.3g|Protein 22.4g|Potassium 208mg|Sodium 14 mg

Storage a sealed container is used to store Chicken Tikka for up to 7 days.

Reheat: just defrost at room temperature for a few hours

13SNACKS & APPETIZERS

13.1 Roasted Pumpkin Seeds

Preparation: 10 minutes
Cooking time: 20 minutes
Servings : 4

Ingredients

- butter, melted -1 1/2 tbsp.(22 g)
- Worcestershire sauce -1/2 tsp (2 ml)
- pumpkin seeds, unwashed -2 cups (276 g)

Preparation

1. Spread the seeds out on a baking sheet after combining 2 cups unwashed pumpkin seeds, 1 1/2 teaspoons melted butter, and 1/2 teaspoon Worcestershire.
2. Bake for about two hours at 250 degrees F (121 degrees C), stirring regularly, until crisp and golden.
3. Serve hot or cold.
4. The seeds can be kept for up to a week if they are kept sealed and completely cooled.

Nutrition Information[per serving]

Calories 412 | Fat 36g | Total Carbohydrate 12.4g | Sugars 0.8g | Protein 17g | Potassium 558mg | Sodium 50 mg

Storage a sealed container is used to store Roasted Pumpkin Seeds for up to 7 days.

Reheat: just defrost at room temperature for a few hours

13.2 Almond Pecan Caramel Popcorn

Preparation: 10 minutes
Cooking time: 60 minutes
Servings : 10

Ingredients

- corn syrup -1/2 cup (155 g)
- baking soda -1 tsp (4 g)
- unblanched almonds -2 cups (284 g)
- pecan halves -1 cup (125 g)
- popped popcorn - 20 cups (480 g)
- unsalted butter -1 cup (227 g)
- brown sugar -1 cup (220 g)
- pinch of cream of tartar

Preparation

1. Spread almonds and pecans equally overcooked popcorn in a big roasting pan.
2. Combine the sugar, butter, corn syrup, and cream of tartar, in a large heavy pot.
3. Over medium-high heat, continuously swirl while bringing to a boil. Allow to boil for five minutes without stirring. After turning off the heat, add the baking soda.
4. After completely covering the popcorn mixture, drizzle caramel over it in a uniform layer.
5. Bake for 1 hour at 200 degrees, stirring every 10 minutes.
6. Allow to cool, stirring occasionally. For up to a week, store in an airtight container.

Nutrition Information[per serving]

Calories 465 | Fat 32.8g | Total Carbohydrate 42.3g | Sugars 19.3g | Protein 5.6g | Potassium 205mg | Sodium 49 mg

Storage a sealed container is used to store Almond Pecan Caramel Popcorn for up to 7 days.

Reheat: just defrost at room temperature for a few hours

13.3 BBQ Winter Squash

Preparation: 10 minutes
Cooking time: 10 minutes
Servings : 8

Ingredients

- olive oil -1-2 tbsp.(15-30 ml)
- brown sugar1-2 tbsp.(15-30 g)
- butternut squash sliced in 1" thick slices -1
- butter1-2 tbsp.(15-30 g)

Preparation

1. the grill should be quite hot (about 400 degrees F) (204 C).
2. Olive oil should be lightly applied to the squash before it is placed on the grill for around five minutes.
3. Brush with melted butter and brown sugar when fork soft.
4. After one minute, remove from grill and serve.

Nutrition Information[per serving]

Calories 36 | Fat 3.2g | Total Carbohydrate 1.7g | Sugars 1.3g | Protein 0.4g | Potassium 66mg | Sodium 11 mg

Storage a sealed container is used to store BBQ Winter Squash for up to 7 days.

Reheat: just defrost at room temperature for a few hours

13.4 Black-Eyed Peas

Preparation: 10 minutes
Cooking time: 90 minutes
Servings : 12

Ingredients

- ginger-1/2 tsp (2 g)
- celery -1 cup (101 g)
- thyme -1/2 tsp (2 g)
- 1 pinch cayenne pepper
- Black-eyed peas, dried -2 cups (242 g)
- onion, finely chopped -1 medium
- water -3 1/2 cups (840 ml)
- curry powder-1/2 tsp (2 g)
- garlic -5 to 6 cloves

Preparation

1. In a large dish, pour enough water to cover the black-eyed peas by 4 inches. Allow to soak for at least six hours or overnight.
2. Cool water should be used to rinse the peas after draining.
3. Fill a large pot with the black-eyed peas and the remaining ingredients.
4. Boil for a few minutes, then reduce heat to low, cover, and boil for 1 1/2 hours until peas are tender.
5. Serve

Nutrition Information[per serving]

Calories 71 | Fat 1.5g | Total Carbohydrate 7.9g | Total Sugars 0.9g | Protein 6.9g | Potassium 186mg | Sodium 146 mg

Storage a sealed container is used to store Black-Eyed Peas for up to 3 days.

Reheat: just defrost at room temperature for a few hours

13.5 Dill Carrots

Preparation: 10 minutes
Cooking time: 05 minutes
Servings : 6

Ingredients

- sugar -3 tbsp. (45 g)
- dill weed -2 tsp (8 g)
- Carrots -1 pound (450 g)
- garlic powder -2 tsp (8 g)
- pepper -1/4 tsp (1 g)
- white vinegar -1 1/2 cups (360 ml)
- plain rice vinegar -1/2 cup (60 ml)

Preparation

1. The carrots should be thinly cut.
2. For three to five minutes, steam in the microwave.
3. Put the carrots in ice water to cool them.
4. Mix the remaining ingredients.
5. Pour onto the carrots.

6. Place there, cover, and refrigerate all night.

Nutrition Information[per serving]
Calories 70 | Fat 0g | Total Carbohydrate 14.7g | Sugars 10.3g | Protein 0.9g | Potassium 308mg | Sodium 56 mg
Storage a sealed container is used to store Dill Carrots for up to 7 days.
Reheat: just defrost at room temperature for a few hours

13.6 Curried Kale

Preparation: 10 minutes
Cooking time:10 minutes
Servings : 4
Ingredients

- Kale -4 cups
- sesame seeds -2 tbsp. (18 g)
- rice vinegar -1/4 cup (15 ml)
- yellow onion -1/2
- turmeric-1 tsp (4 g)
- Oil -1 tbsp.(15 ml)
- curry powder -1 tsp (4 g)
- water -1/2 cup (120 ml)

Preparation

1. Remove the tough centre after washing the kale. Slice lengthwise into long strips, then make crosscuts every three inches.
2. In oil, sauté onion till transparent. Add the curry powder and the turmeric, and roast for about a minute.
3. Include water or chicken broth and kale. Cover while keeping an eye on. Add 1/4 cup water if extra liquid is required.
4. Continue to cover and stir regularly until the kale wilts and turns bright green. Avoid overcooking as it will get very black.
5. Take out the kale from the pan, reserving the juices.
6. Include sesame seeds, rice vinegar, and soy sauce. Stir continuously until

sesame seeds begin to pop and sauce thickens.
7. Pour sesame oil over the greens after taking the pan off the heat.

Nutrition Information[per serving]
Calories 108 | Fat 5.8g | Total Carbohydrate 10g | Sugars 0.6g | Protein 3.1g | Potassium 392mg | Sodium 31 mg
Storage a sealed container is used to store Curried Kale for up to 7 days.
Reheat: just defrost at room temperature for a few hours

13.7 Creamy Strawberry Snacks

Preparation: 10 minutes
Cooking time: 00 minutes
Servings : 3
Ingredients

- Crackers -12
- whipped mixed berry cream cheese spread -1/4 cup (40 g)
- strawberries -3 medium

Preparation

1. One spoonful of cream cheese spread should be used to cover each cracker.
2. Add a strawberry or piece of fruit on top.
3. Serve right away.
4. Mix 3 tablespoons of protein powder with the cream cheese for a higher protein option.

Nutrition Information[per serving]
Calories 364 | Fat 18.1g | Total Carbohydrate 43.7g | Sugars 7.3g | Protein 4.1g | Potassium 18mg | Sodium 174 mg
Storage a sealed container is used to store Creamy Strawberry Snacks for up to 7 days.
Reheat: just defrost at room temperature for a few hours

13.8 Blasted Brussels Sprouts

Preparation: 10 minutes
Cooking time: 10 minutes
Servings : 6

Ingredients

- Brussels Sprouts (about one stalk) -2 cups (176 g)
- Parmesan Cheese -2-4 tablespoons (28 – 56 g)
- fruit or herb flavoured vinegar -1/4 cup (15 ml)
- olive oil -1-2 tablespoons (15-30 ml)

Preparation

1. Oven should be heated to 450 degrees F (232 degrees C).
2. Remove any fallen leaves. Leave tiny sprouts whole and slice larger sprouts in half.
3. Mix olive oil with the sprouts.
4. Place on a baking sheet that has been lightly greased.
5. 10 minutes for roasting. When soft enough to puncture with a fork, sprouts are finished.
6. After taking it out of the oven, top it with freshly grated Parmesan cheese and fruit vinegar.

Nutrition Information[per serving]

Calories 66|Fat 4.9g|Total Carbohydrate 3g|Sugars 0.3g|Protein 4g|Potassium 114mg|Sodium 94 mg

Storage a sealed container is used to store Blasted Brussels Sprouts for up to 7 days.

Reheat: just defrost at room temperature for a few hours

13.9 Dilled Cream Cheese Spread

Preparation: 10 minutes
Cooking time: 00 minutes
Servings : 8

Ingredients

- whipped cream cheese -8 ounces (225 g)
- fresh dill, -1/2 tsp (2 g)
- onion powder -1 tsp (4 g)

Preparation

1. Combine all the ingredients completely using an electric mixer.
2. Store in an airtight container in the refrigerator.

Nutrition Information

Calories 28|Fat 0.4 g|Total Carbohydrate 1.9g|Sugars 0.2g|Protein 4.1g|Potassium 51mg|Sodium 154 mg

Storage a sealed container is used to store Dilled Cream Cheese Spread for up to 7 days.

Reheat: just defrost at room temperature for a few hours

13.10 Easy Blueberry-Lemon Parfait

Preparation: 10 minutes
Cooking time: 00 minutes
Servings : 4

Ingredients

- blueberries, fresh or thawed frozen -2 cups (290 g)
- gingersnaps, crumbled -10
- coconut yogurt -2 (8 ounce) (450 g)

Preparation

1. 1/4 cup blueberries, 1/4 cup yoghurt, and 1/4 cup of crushed gingersnaps should be placed in four dishes, wine glasses, or mason jars.
2. Repeat to layer each component twice.

Nutrition Information[per serving]

Calories 195|Fat 3.4g|Total Carbohydrate 31.9g|Sugars 18.3g|Protein 8g|Potassium 382mg|Sodium 194 mg

Storage a sealed container is used to store Easy Blueberry-Lemon Parfait for up to 1-2 days.

Reheat: just defrost at room temperature for a few hours

13.11 Edamole Spread

Preparation: 10 minutes
Cooking time: 00 minutes
Servings: 6

Ingredients

- Water -3 tbsp. (45 ml)
- parsley leaves -1/4 cup (15 g)
- Edamame -3/4 cup (56 g)
- lemon rind, grated finely -1 tbsp.(15 g)
- lemon juice-1 tbsp.(15 ml)
- garlic clove -1
- olive oil -2 tbsp. (30 ml)

Preparation

1. Add all ingredients and pulse until thoroughly incorporated in a food processor or blender.
2. Cover, then allow to stand.
3. Accompany with tortilla chips or slices of pita.

Nutrition Information[per serving]

Calories 73|Fat 5.9g|Total Carbohydrate 3.1g|Sugars 0.4g|Protein 3.4g|Potassium 123mg|Sodium 5mg

Storage a sealed container is used to store Edamole Spread for up to 7 days.

Reheat: just defrost at room temperature for a few hours

13.12 Fruit Salsa

Preparation: 10 minutes
Cooking time: 00 minutes
Servings : 4

Ingredients

- red onion, diced -1/4 cup (40 g)
- honey or brown sugar (optional) -2 tbsp. (30 g)
- lime juice -3-4 tbsp. (45 ml)
- fresh mint leaves, cilantro or basil, chopped -2 tbsp. (8 g)
- Pineapple -3/4 cup (123 g)
- strawberries, raspberries, or blueberries, diced -1 cup (145 g)
- jalapeño -1

Preparation

1. All the ingredients should be combined and stirred in a medium ceramic or glass bowl.
2. Before serving, let the salsa marinate for 20 to 30 minutes covered in plastic wrap.
3. Depending on how sweet the fruit is, taste and adjust the amount of lime juice and honey (if used).
4. Serve with fajitas, fish, chicken, or pork..

Nutrition Information[per serving]

Calories 81|Fat 0.2g|Total Carbohydrate 21.7g|Sugars 16.3g |Protein 0.8g|Potassium 127mg|Sodium 2 mg

Storage a sealed container is used to store Fruit Salsa for up to 2 days.

Reheat: just defrost at room temperature for a few hours

13.13 Green Beans with Hazelnuts and Dried Cranberries

Preparation: 10 minutes
Cooking time: 15 minutes
Servings: 8

Ingredients

- dried cranberries -1/2 cup (25 g)
- hazelnuts -1/2 cup (57 g)
- water -12 cups (2880 ml)
- shallots -1/3 cup (20 g)
- lemon zest -1/2 tsp (2 g)
- olive oil - 3 tbsp. (45 ml)
- fresh (or frozen) green beans -1 1/2 pounds (680 g)

Preparation

1. Set the oven to 350 degrees Fahrenheit and turn it on (176 C).
2. Place the hazelnuts in a single layer on a baking sheet. Bake at 350°F for 13 minutes, or until the skins begin to separate.
3. To remove the skins, put the torched nuts in a sieve or dish and vigorously wipe them with a towel. Roughly cut the nuts.
4. Bring 12 cups of water to a rolling boil in a large pot. When the potatoes are crisp-tender, add the beans and simmer for 4 minutes. Drain, then immerse in freezing water before repeating the procedure. Beans should be dried using a towel.
5. Heat a sizable skillet to medium. Stir the oil into the pan to coat it. Shallots are added, and they are cooked until they barely start to brown. Boil the beans for three minutes with frequent stirring after adding them. 1 minute after the addition of the cranberries and hazelnuts. Sprinkle some lemon zest on top.

Nutrition Information[per serving]

Calories 113|Fat 8.4g |Total Carbohydrate 9.3g|Sugars 1.8g |Protein 2.4g|Potassium 194mg|Sodium 12 mg

Storage a sealed container is used to store Green Beans with Hazelnuts and Dried Cranberries for up to 7 days.

Reheat: just defrost at room temperature for a few hours

13.14 Grilled Portobello Mushrooms

Preparation: 10 minutes
Cooking time: 10 minutes
Servings : 6

Ingredients

- brown sugar -1/3 cup (48 g)
- shallots -1/2 cup (20 g)

- Portobello mushrooms -3 large
- lite-sodium soy sauce -2 tsp (8 ml)
- sesame oil -1/8 cup (30 ml)
- balsamic vinegar -1/8 cup (30 ml)

Preparation

1. Set cleaned mushrooms aside in step one.
2. In a small baking dish, combine the remaining ingredients. Place the marinated mushrooms in the platter and refrigerate overnight.
3. Grill mushrooms for 5 minutes on each side, or until they are dark.
4. Mushrooms will shrink when cooked.

Nutrition Information[per serving]

Calories 92|Fat 4.6g |Total Carbohydrate 11.9g|Sugars 7.9g|Protein 1.9g|Potassium 212mg|Sodium 63 mg

Storage a sealed container is used to store Grilled Portobello Mushrooms for up to 3-5 days.

Reheat: just defrost at room temperature for a few hours

13.15 Quick Pesto

Preparation: 10 minutes
Cooking time: 00 minutes
Servings : 8

Ingredients

- grated parmesan cheese -10 tbsp. (141 g)
- walnuts -2 tbsp. (16 g)
- olive oil -2/3 cup (160 ml)
- fresh basil leaves -40
- garlic -1 clove

Preparation

1. All ingredients—except the oil—should be finely ground in a food processor or blender.
2. Add oil gradually while the motor is running until it is well-combined.
3. savour with hot spaghetti.

Nutrition Information[per serving]
Calories 270|Fat 25.5g|Total Carbohydrate 1.7g|Sugars 0g|Protein 11.4g|Potassium 19mg|Sodium 325 mg

Storage a sealed container is used to store Quick Pesto for up to 7 days.

Reheat: just defrost at room temperature for a few hours

13.16 Rosemary-Sage Crackers

Preparation: 10 minutes
Cooking time: 10 minutes
Servings: 12

Ingredients

- fresh Parmesan cheese, finely shredded -2 tbsp. and 1/3 cup (28 g+ 75 g)
- whole-wheat flour -1/3 cup (11 g)
- olive oil -1 tbsp. (15 ml)
- garlic powder -1 tsp (4 g)
- rosemary, -1 tbsp. (5 g)
- sage -1 tbsp. (4 g)
- water -1/2 cup (120 ml)
- vegetable oil -3 tbsp. (45 ml)
- all-purpose flour -1 1/4 cups (156 g)

Preparation

1. Set the oven to 350 degrees Fahrenheit and turn it on (176 C).
2. Combine the whole-wheat flour, all-purpose flour, chopped herbs, and 2 tablespoons of parmesan cheese in a medium bowl.
3. In the centre of the flour mixture, create a well.
4. Fill the well with water and vegetable oil.
5. Blend thoroughly using a fork.
6. Roll out the dough on a lightly dusted surface to a thickness of no more than 1/8 inch.
7. After transferring the dough to a baking sheet that hasn't been oiled, cut the dough into 1 1/2 inch squares by cutting halfway through.
8. Insert the fork roughly three times into each square.
9. Rub dough with olive oil.
10. Sprinkle over some garlic powder and a third cup of parmesan cheese.
11. Bake for 15 to 20 minutes, or until crisp and golden brown.
12. Separate into individual crackers after let to cool.

Nutrition Information[per serving]
Calories 148|Fat 6.1g |Total Carbohydrate 19.2g|Sugars 0.1g|Protein 4.6g|Potassium 64mg|Sodium 3 mg

Storage a sealed container is used to store Rosemary-Sage Crackers for up to 7 days.

Reheat: just defrost at room temperature for a few hours

13.17 Spiced Almonds and Cashews

Preparation: 10 minutes
Cooking time: 15 minutes
Servings : 5

Ingredients

- raw almonds -1/2 cup (71 g)
- garlic powder -1/4 tsp (1 g)
- low sodium soy sauce- 1 tbsp. (15 ml)
- Worcestershire sauce -1/2 tsp (2 ml)
- onion powder-1/4 tsp (1 g)
- raw cashews -1/2 cup (68 g)
- ground cumin-1/4 tsp (1 g)

Preparation

1. Oven should be heated to 300 degrees F (148 C).
2. On a baking sheet, evenly distribute the nuts.
3. Bake cashews for 13 minutes or until gently browned.
4. The remaining ingredients should be combined in a small bowl in the meanwhile.
5. Toss the roasted nuts with the spice mixture to distribute the coating.

6. Return the coated nuts to the oven for an additional five minutes to set the flavour.
7. Use an airtight container for storage. Keep in the refrigerator if you plan to keep it for longer than a few days.

Nutrition Information[per serving]

Calories 137|Fat 11.1g|Total Carbohydrate 7.2g|Sugars 1.3g |Protein 4.4g|Potassium 159 mg|Sodium 124 mg

Storage a sealed container is used to store Spiced Almonds and Cashews for up to 7 days.

Reheat: just defrost at room temperature for a few hours

13.18 Sweet Potato Fries

Preparation: 10 minutes

Cooking time: 14 minutes

Servings : 8

Ingredients

- non-stick cooking spray - 1tsp .
- sweet potatoes -4

Preparation

1. Oven should be heated to 500 degrees F (260 C).
2. Sliced sweet potatoes should be 1/8" thick after being peeled (soak to lower the potassium).
3. Use salad oil to clean or nonstick cooking spray to coat cookie sheet.
4. Bake for 15 minutes after placing on a baking sheet.

Nutrition Information[per serving]

Calories 60|Fat 1.1g|Total Carbohydrate 11.7g|Sugars 3.5g|Protein 1g|Potassium 0 mg|Sodium 35 mg

Storage a sealed container is used to store Sweet Potato Fries for up to 7 days.

Reheat: just defrost at room temperature for a few hours

13.19 Spicy Crunch and Munch Snack Mix

Preparation: 10 minutes

Cooking time: 60 minutes

Servings : 20

Ingredients

- cayenne pepper -1/8 tsp (1/2 g)
- lemon juice-1-1/2 tsp (6 ml)
- unsalted pretzel twists -1 cup (30 g)
- unsalted transfat-free margarine -5 tbsp. (70 g)
- Ralston Purina® Rice Chex® cereal -4 cups (120 g)
- chili powder -1 tbsp. (15 g)
- ground cumin -1/4 tsp (1 g)
- Kellogg's® Crispex® cereal -2 cups (100 g)
- Worcestershire sauce -1-1/2 tsp (6 ml)
- garlic powder -1/2 tsp (2 g)
- bite-sized oyster crackers -3 cups (100 g)

Preparation

1. Adjust the oven to 250°F (121 C).
2. In a 10- by 15-inch pan, melted the margarine. Lemon juice, seasonings, and Worcestershire sauce ought to be included.
3. You should add cereal, crackers, and pretzels. Evenly coat by tossing.
4. After 45 minutes of baking, carefully stir once every 15 minutes.
5. To cool, spread out on paper towels.
6. Keep the container airtight.

Nutrition Information[per serving]

Calories 60|Fat 0.9g|Total Carbohydrate 11.9g| Sugars 1.9g |Protein 1.1g|Potassium 28mg|Sodium 114 mg

Storage a sealed container is used to store Spicy Crunch and Munch Snack Mix for up to 7 days.

Reheat: just defrost at room temperature for a few hours

13.20 Sweet and Spicy Tortilla Chips

Preparation: 10 minutes

Cooking time: 10 minutes

Servings : 8

Ingredients

- ground cumin-1/2 tsp (2 g)
- ground cayenne pepper -1/4 tsp (1 g)
- brown sugar -1 tsp (4 g)
- garlic powder-1/2 tsp (2 g)
- ground chili powder -1/2 tsp (2 g)
- flour tortillas, 6" size -6
- Butter -1/4 cup (56 g)

Preparation

1. Set your oven to 425 F. (218 C).
2. Cooking oil should be sprayed on a baking sheet.
3. In a separate bowl, mix the spices, brown sugar, and melted butter.
4. Each tortilla should be divided into eight wedges. On the baking sheet, arrange the wedges in a single layer.
5. Apply the spice mixture to the tortillas with a pastry brush.
6. When browned, bake for 8 minutes. To be served hot or cold.
7. Put additional chips in an airtight container to keep them fresh.

Nutrition Information

Calories 96| Fat 6.3 g|Total Carbohydrate 8.6 g|Sugars 0.6 g |Protein 1.2 g|Potassium 41mg|Sodium 49 mg

Storage a sealed container is used to store Sweet and Spicy Tortilla Chips for up to 7 days.

Reheat: just defrost at room temperature for a few hours

14DESSERTS

14.1 Healthy Cinnamon Carrot Cookies

Preparation: 10 minutes
Cooking time: 15 minutes
Servings :12

Ingredients

- Ground Cinnamon -2 tsp (8 g)
- Maple Syrup/Honey -½ Cup (158 g)
- Grated Carrot -1 Cup (110 g)
- All Spice -½ tsp (2 g)
- Vanilla Extract -2 tsp (8 g)
- Eggs -2
- Brown Rice Flour -½ Cup (79 g)
- 1g salt -⅛ tsp (1/2 g)
- Rolled Oats gluten free -1 ¼ Cup (60 g)
- Baking Powder -2 tsp (8 g)
- melted Coconut Oil -½ Cup (100 g)

Preparation

1. Then, preheat the oven to 180 °C and line a baking sheet with parchment paper (82 C).
2. All spices, cinnamon, salt, baking powder, brown rice flour, and oats should be combined with the nutmeg.
3. Combine the maple syrup/honey, vanilla, coconut oil, and egg in a mixing bowl fitted with a paddle attachment.
4. After incorporating the dry ingredients, you should keep mixing in the liquid ones. Don't forget the veggies.
5. Refrigerate the batter for twenty minutes.
6. Dollop the dough onto the baking sheet in 12 equal rounds, and then lightly push it down.
7. 15 minutes of baking
8. Let it cool.

Nutrition Information[per serving]

Calories 193|Fat 10.8 g|Total Carbohydrate 22.9 g|Total Sugars 9.1 g|Protein 3 g|Potassium 173mg|Sodium 30 mg

Storage a sealed container is used to store Healthy Cinnamon Carrot Cookies for up to 7 days.

Reheat: just defrost at room temperature for a few hours

14.2 Roasted Cinnamon Pineapple

Preparation: 10 minutes
Cooking time: 15 minutes
Servings : 6

Ingredients

- fresh lime juice -1 tbsp. (15 ml)
- Lime zest (optional)
- Butter -2 tbsp. (30 g)
- cinnamon -1 tsp (4 g)
- Honey -1/4 cup (84 g)
- Pineapple -1

Preparation

1. Set your oven to 425 F. (218 C).
2. Cut the ends off the pineapple. Cut the fruit into six wedges, each measuring an inch, after peeling and coring.
3. Spray nonstick cooking spray and foil with foil on a baking sheet with a rim.
4. Melt the butter in a small bowl and add the lime juice, honey, and cinnamon.
5. Place the pineapple wedges flat side down in the baking dish. Distribute the half of the sauce over the wedges in an equal layer. Use the remaining sauce to repeat the process on the other side of the wedges.

6. Roast pineapple in the oven for 10 minutes on a baking sheet. The pineapple wedges should be lightly toasted and caramelised after fifteen minutes after turning them over.

7. Serve the dish hot and gently allow it to cool. Garnish with lime zest.

Nutrition Information[per serving]

Calories 93 | Fat 3.8 g | Total Carbohydrate 16.1 g | Total Sugars 14.2 g | Protein0.4g | Potassium 19mg | Sodium 31 mg

Storage a sealed container is used to store Roasted Cinnamon Pineapple for up to 2 days.

Reheat: just defrost at room temperature for a few hours

14.3 Peach Cobbler

Preparation: 10 minutes
Cooking time: 45 minutes
Servings : 12

Ingredients

- ground cinnamon -1/2 tsp (2 g)
- Splenda® No Calorie Sweetener, granulated -2/3 cup (134 g)
- almond milk (original flavor) -1 cup (240 ml)
- baking powder -1/2 tbsp. (8 g)
- all purpose flour -1 cup (125 g)
- canned peach pie filling -20 ounces (566 g)
- unsalted butter -6 tbsp. (90 g)

Preparation

1. Set the oven to 350 degrees Fahrenheit (176 C).
2. Splenda® (or sugar), baking powder, flour, and almond milk, should be thoroughly combined in a large bowl. Set aside.
3. Melt butter in a microwave-safe basin before pouring it into a 9" x 13" baking dish.
4. Pour the milk mixture on top of the butter that has just melted into the baking dish.

5. Using a large spoon, distribute the open pie filling in a haphazard pattern over the batter in the baking dish.
6. Cinnamon powder should be added to the cobbler's top.
7. Bake the crust for 43 minutes, or until it is puffy and golden.

Nutrition Information[per serving]

Calories 186 | Fat 10.6 g | Total Carbohydrate 24.4 g | Sugars 10.7 g | Protein 1.6 g | Potassium 130 mg | Sodium 67 mg

Storage a sealed container is used to store Peach Cobbler for up to 7 days.

Reheat: just defrost at room temperature for a few hours

14.4 Apple Crisp

Preparation: 10 minutes
Cooking time: 10 minutes
Servings : 12

Ingredients

- brown sugar -3/4 cup (165 g)
- cinnamon -1 tsp (4 g)
- unsalted butter -1/2 cup (113 g)
- baking powder -1/4 tsp (1 g)
- oatmeal -1 cup (81 g)
- granulated sugar -1/2 cup (100 g)
- all-purpose flour -1-1/4 cups (156 g)
- Apples -5
- baking soda -1/4 tsp (1 g)

Preparation

1. Set the oven's temperature to 350 F. (176 C).
2. Cooking spray needs to be used to a 9 x 9-inch pan.
3. Apples need to be cored, peeled, and cut into slices.
4. Combine 1/2 cup of granulated sugar, 1/2 teaspoon of cinnamon, and. 3 tablespoons of flour. After including the apple bits, combine.
5. Add the apple mixture to the pan after preparation.

6. Combine the baking powder, baking soda, cinnamon, brown sugar, oats, flour, and in a larger basin. Use a fork or pastry blender to stir the butter into the mixture.

7. After placing the apples on top, bake the dish for an hour..

Nutrition Information[per serving]

Calories 246|Fat 8.4 g|Total Carbohydrate 42.8 g|Sugars 26 g|Protein 2.2 g|Potassium 161mg|Sodium 86 mg

Storage a sealed container is used to store Apple Crisp for up to 7 days.

Reheat: just defrost at room temperature for a few hours

14.5 Pumpkin Cheesecake Bars

Preparation: 10 minutes

Cooking time: 30 minutes

Servings : 16

Ingredients

- ground cinnamon -1-1/2 tsp (6 g)
- vanilla extract-1 tsp (4 g)
- Butter -5 tbsp. (75 g)
- eggs -2
- cream cheese -8 ounces (226 g)
- pureed pumpkin -1/2 cup (60 g)
- granulated sugar -3/4 cup (150 g)
- ground allspice -1 tsp (4 g)
- all-purpose flour -1 cup (125 g)
- golden brown sugar -1/3 cup (74 g)

Preparation

1. Set the oven to 425 F (218 C).
2. Butter and cream cheese should be out for melting.
3. Flour and brown sugar should be combined in a medium bowl. To make a crumb mixture, cut in butter.
4. Reserve 3/4 cup of the ingredients for the topping. The remainder of the mixture should be pressed into an 8" by 8" by 1-1/2" baking tray.
5. After 15 minutes of baking, remove from oven. Cool a little.

6. Lightly whisk the egg. Vanilla, ground allspice, cinnamon, eggs, pumpkin, cream cheese, and sugar (or sugar replacement) should be combined in a large mixing dish. Put everything in a blender and whir it around until it's completely smooth.

7. Apply the mixture to the cooked crust. Add the saved topping on top.

8. Add another 30 to 35 minutes of baking.

9. Before cutting into bars, let cool.

Nutrition Information[per serving]

Calories 170|Fat 9.3 g|Total Carbohydrate 19.6 g|Total Sugars 12.6 g|Protein 2.9 g|Potassium 41mg|Sodium 78 mg

Storage a sealed container is used to store Pumpkin Cheesecake Bars for up to 7 days.

Reheat: just defrost at room temperature for a few hours

14.6 Apple Cake

Preparation: 10 minutes

Cooking time: 75 minutes

Servings : 16

Ingredients

- all-purpose white flour -3 cups (375 g)
- canola oil -1 cup (240 ml)
- baking powder -1 tbsp. (5 g)
- orange juice -1/4 cup (60 ml)
- eggs -4
- vanilla extract -2-1/2 tsp (10 g)
- Apples -6
- Cinnamon -2 tsp (8 g)
- Sugar -2-1/3 cups (266 g)

Preparation

1. Set the oven to 425 F (218 C).
2. Apply nonstick cooking spray to a tube pan.
3. Slice or chop apples after they have been cored and peeled.
4. 1/3 cup sugar and cinnamon are combined. Add the apple and combine.

5. The rest of the ingredients should be mixed together in a basin and then blended smooth using an electric mixer.
6. Before adding the remaining cake batter, place the apple slices in the prepared tube pan.
7. 75 minutes in the oven, or until golden brown and a toothpick inserted into the centre comes out clean.

Nutrition Information[per serving]
Calories 366|Fat 15.3 g|Total Carbohydrate 55.6 g|Total Sugars 34.6 g|Protein 4.2 g|Potassium 236 mg|Sodium 20 mg

Storage a sealed container is used to store Apple Cake for up to 7 days.

Reheat: just defrost at room temperature for a few hours

14.7 Easy Pumpkin Cheesecake

Preparation: 10 minutes
Cooking time: 50 minutes
Servings : 8
Ingredients

- pumpkin puree -1/2 cup (122 g)
- egg white -1
- granulated sugar -1/2 cup (100 g)
- vanilla extract -1 tsp (4 g)
- liquid egg substitute -1/2 cup (125 g)
- Nabisco® 'Nilla® wafer crumb 9" pie crust -1
- pumpkin pie spice -1 tsp (4 g)
- cream cheese -16 ounces (450 g)
- frozen dessert topping -8 tbsp. (32 g)

Preparation
1. Turn the oven on to 375°F (190 C). Apply egg white to pie crust and bake for five minutes. 350°F (176 C) is a good oven temperature to use.
2. Mix sugar, vanilla, and softened cream cheese in a sizable bowl until smooth, using a mixer at high speed.

3. Add egg substitute by beating. Blend till smooth after including pumpkin puree and pumpkin pie spice.
4. Fill the pie crust with the pumpkin mixture and bake for 45 minutes until the center is firm. After chilling the pie,
5. Slice into 8 pieces. Serve 1 spoonful of dessert topping on top of each slice.

Nutrition Information[per serving]
Calories 286|Fat 21.3 g|Total Carbohydrate 15.6 g|Sugars 14.6 g|Protein 6.9 g|Potassium 134mg|Sodium 219 mg

Storage a sealed container is used to store Easy Pumpkin Cheesecake for up to 7 days.

Reheat: just defrost at room temperature for a few hours

14.8 Muffins

Preparation: 10 minutes
Cooking time: 20 minutes
Servings : 12
Ingredients

- cinnamon -1-1/2 tsp (6 g)
- baking soda -1 tsp (4 g)
- sugar -1 cup (200 g)
- canola oil -1/2 cup (120 ml)
- muffin papers -12
- water -1/4 cup (60 ml)
- vanilla -1 tbsp. (4 g)
- raw apple -1-1/2 cups (165 g)
- all purpose white flour -1-1/2 cups (188 g)
- eggs -2

Preparation
1. Place muffin liners in the pan, and preheat the oven to 400 degrees Fahrenheit (204 C). Apple should be peeled and then chopped into small pieces.
2. In an enormous bowl, beat the eggs. After adding the sugar, oil, and water, thoroughly combine. include vanilla

3. Combine the flour, baking soda, and 1 teaspoon of cinnamon in a different basin.
4. Incorporate the egg mixture into the flour mixture. It will be lumpy batter. Add the apple chunks and fold.
5. Cups must be approximately 3/4 full. 1 teaspoon sugar and 1/2 teaspoon cinnamon should be combined. Sprinkle on top of the muffins.
6. Bake for 20 minutes, or until just lightly browned on top.

Nutrition Information[per serving]
Calories 228|Fat 6.3 g|Total Carbohydrate 31 g| Sugars 0.6 g|Protein 3g|Potassium 35 mg|Sodium 119 mg

Storage a sealed container is used to store Muffins for up to 7 days.

Reheat: just defrost at room temperature for a few hours

14.9 Cherry Coffee Cake

Preparation: 10 minutes
Cooking time: 40 minutes
Servings : 24

Ingredients

- granulated sugar -1 cup (200 g)
- cherry pie filling -20 ounces (566 g)
- baking powder -1 tsp (4 g)
- all-purpose white flour -2 cups (250 g)
- unsalted butter -1/2 cup (113 g)
- vanilla -1 tsp (4 g)
- eggs -2
- sour cream -1 cup (230 g)
- baking soda -1 tsp (4 g)

Preparation

1. Adjust the oven's heat to 350 degrees Fahrenheit (176 C). Butter should be left out to soften at room temperature.
2. Put the butter, eggs, sugar, sour cream, and vanilla in a mixer.

3. Combine the baking powder, soda, and flour in a separate basin.
4. After adding the dry ingredients, thoroughly combine them with the butter mixture that has been creamed. Fill a 9-by-13-inch baking dish with batter.
5. Scatter cherry pie filling evenly over the batter.
6. Beautiful golden after 40 minutes of baking

Nutrition Information [per serving]
Calories 157|Fat 6.3 g|Total   Carbohydrate 23.6 g|Sugars 8.6 g|Protein 2 g|Potassium 77 mg|Sodium 94 mg

Storage a sealed container is used to store Cherry Coffee Cake for up to 7 days.

Reheat: just defrost at room temperature for a few hours

14.10 Arroz Con Leche

Preparation: 10 minutes
Cooking time: 20 minutes
Servings : 6

Ingredients

- granulated sugar -1/4 cup (50 g)
- almond milk, unsweetened -2 cups (480 ml)
- cinnamon -1/4 tsp (1 g)
- vanilla extract -1 tsp (4 g)
- raisins -2 tbsp. (40 g)
- white rice, uncooked -1 cup (185 g)
-

Preparation

1. After washing the rice with tap water, drain it.
2. In a medium-sized saucepan, combine the rice and 1 cup of water. After coming to a boil, simmer for 10 minutes while covered.
3. After taking off the lid, add almond milk and raisins. Boil the rice for 10 minutes, or until it is cooked, once again covering the pot. Not all of the

liquid will boil out, leaving the rice to resemble soup.

4. After the rice has done cooking, remove it from the fire and stir in the sugar, cinnamon, and vanilla (or sugar replacement). Well combine, then warmly serve.

5. Keep any leftovers in the fridge.

Nutrition Information[per serving]

Calories 339|Fat 19.3 g|Total Carbohydrate 40 g|Sugars 0.6 g|Protein 1.2 g|Potassium 41mg|Sodium 49 mg

Storage a sealed container is used to store Sweet and Spicy Tortilla Chips for up to 7 days.

Reheat: just defrost at room temperature for a few hours

14.11 Strawberry Pudding

Preparation: 10 minutes
Cooking time: 05 minutes
Servings : 6

Ingredients

- lemon zest -1 tsp (4 g)
- Strawberries -2 cups (288 g)
- Sugar -1/2 cup (100 g)
- whipped dessert topping -6 tbsp.(54 g)
- fresh lemon juice -1 tbsp. (15 ml)
- corn-starch -2-1/2 tbsp. (10 g)
- Water -1 cup (240 ml)

Preparation

1. Smash strawberries.
2. Water is brought to a boil. Add sugar and mix. Add crushed strawberries to the sugar water that is now boiling, then simmer gently. Lemon zest and juice should be added. 3 minutes of simmering the mixture while stirring.
3. Strawberries are coated with a mixture of cornflour and a little cold water. About 1 to 2 minutes of stirring and cooking will thicken the mixture. Get rid of the heat.
4. Mixture should be divided among six dessert dishes and cooled in the fridge.

5. Add 1 tablespoon of whipped topping to each plate before serving.

Nutrition Information[per serving]

Calories 112|Fat 2.2 g|Total Carbohydrate 24.6 g|Sugars 19.6 g|Protein 0.4 g|Potassium 78 mg|Sodium 5 mg

Storage a sealed container is used to store Strawberry Pudding for up to 7 days.

Reheat: just defrost at room temperature for a few hours

14.12 Fudge

Preparation: 10 minutes
Cooking time: 10 minutes
Servings : 18

Ingredients

- half & half creamer -2/3 cup (162 g)
- semi-sweet chocolate chips -1-1/2 cups (42 g)
- granulated sugar -1-2/3 cups (334 g)
- vanilla extract -1 tsp (4 g)
- miniature marshmallows -1-1/2 cups (45 g)

Preparation

1. Use nonstick spray or butter to grease a 9" square pan.
2. In a big, heavy pot, mix the half-and-half and sugar. After bringing to a boil, gently lower heat. For five minutes, maintain a rolling boil while stirring continuously.
3. Add the marshmallows, chocolate chips, and vanilla essence after taking the pan from the heat. It is necessary to heat marshmallows while stirring them.
4. Quickly pour into a pan with butter. Cut into 18 pieces, each 3" x 1-1/2" long after cooling.

Nutrition Information[per serving]

Calories 68|Fat 1.5 g |Total Carbohydrate 13.6 g|Sugars 12.6 g|Protein 0.4 g|Potassium 12 mg|Sodium 5 mg

Storage a sealed container is used to store Fudge for up to 7 days.

Reheat: just defrost at room temperature for a few hours

14.13 Blueberry Whipped Pie

Preparation: 10 minutes

Cooking time: 10 minutes

Servings : 9

Ingredients

- granulated sugar -1/4 cup (60 g)
- blueberries -3 cups (435 g)
- vanilla extract -1 tsp (4 g)
- tub non dairy whipped cream -8 ounce (226 g)
- unsalted butter, melted -1/2 cup (120 g)
- cream cheese, softened -8 ounces (226 g)
- lemon juice -2 tsp (8 ml)
- cinnamon -1 tsp (4 g)
- graham cracker crumbs -2 cups

Preparation

1. Turn on the 375 degrees F (190 C)oven.
2. The melted butter, cinnamon, and graham cracker crumb should be mixed in a medium bowl.
3. To create a crust, press the mixture firmly into the bottom of a 9-inch round or square baking dish.
4. 7 minutes in the oven, then allow the crust cool.
5. Cream cheese that has been softened and sugar should be combined smoothly in a big bowl using an electric mixer.
6. Lemon juice and vanilla extract are combined.
7. Fold in the blueberries after carefully incorporating the whipped topping.
8. Over the crust, evenly distribute the mixture.
9. Cover and chill the food in the refrigerator for at least an hour.

Nutrition Information[per serving]

Calories 337 | Fat 21 g | Total Carbohydrate 34 g | Sugars 19.6 g | Protein 3.6 g | Potassium 104 mg | Sodium 314 mg

Storage a sealed container is used to store Blueberry Whipped Pie for up to 7 days.

Reheat: just defrost at room temperature for a few hours

14.14 Sweet Custard

Preparation: 10 minutes

Cooking time:05 minutes

Servings: 4

Ingredients

- Sugar -2 tbsp. (12 g)
- Eggs -4
- vanilla extract -1/2 tsp (2 g)
- Almond Milk -1 cup (240 ml)

Preparation

1. Increase the oven's temperature to 325 F (162 C).
2. Everything needs to be combined completely.
3. Divide the batter into 4 lightly oiled custard cups.
4. After placing the custard cups inside the baking pan, add hot water to the pan until it comes halfway up the sides of the cups.
5. After the custard has cooked for about an hour, a knife inserted close to the centre should come out clean.
6. Before serving, let the food stand for five minutes.
7. Heat the custard in the bowls in the microwave for seven minutes on low power, rotating the dishes as necessary to ensure even heating.

Nutrition Information[per serving]

Calories 117 | Fat 5.6 g | Total Carbohydrate 9.4 g | Sugars 9.2 g | Protein 7.5 g | Potassium 95 mg | Sodium 90 mg

1510 WEEKS MEAL PLAN

15.1 Week 1

Day	Breakfast	Lunch	Dinner	Snacks	Dessert
1	Deviled eggs	Mushroom Soup	Quick and Easy Chicken Stir-Fry	**Easy Blueberry-Lemon Parfait**	Sweet Custard
2	Dilly Scrambled Eggs	Simple Cabbage Soup	Parmesan roasted cauliflower	**Creamy Strawberry Snacks**	Blueberry Whipped Pie
3	Loaded Veggie Eggs			**Dill Carrots**	Fudge
4	Easy Apple Oatmeal	Chicken Wild Rice Asparagus Soup	Linguine with Garlic and Shrimp	**Almond Pecan Caramel Popcorn**	Strawberry Pudding
5	Egg White French Toast	Summer zucchini "lasagna	Eggplant and Tofu Stir-Fry	**Sweet Potato Fries**	Arroz Con Leche
6	Omelettes	Red Lentil Dahl	Fruit Salad Slaw	**Grilled Portobello Mushrooms**	Cherry Coffee Cake
7	Blueberry Muffins	Maple syrup sage carrots	Chicken Salad	**Fruit Salsa**	Muffins

15.2 Week 2

Day	Breakfast	Lunch	Dinner	Snacks	Dessert
1	**Tofu and Kale scramble**	Quick and Easy Chicken Stir-Fry	Mushroom Soup	**Spiced Almonds and Cashews**	**Easy Pumpkin Cheesecake**
2	**Energy Bars**	Parmesan roasted cauliflower	Simple Cabbage Soup	**Sweet Potato Fries**	**Apple Cake**
3	**Eccentric Taste**			**Spicy Crunch and Munch Snack Mix**	**Pumpkin Cheesecake Bars**
4	**Blueberry Blast Smoothie**	Linguine with Garlic and Shrimp	Chicken Wild Rice Asparagus Soup	**Sweet and Spicy Tortilla Chips**	**Apple Crisp**
5	**Strawberry mockarita**	Eggplant and Tofu Stir-Fry	Summer zucchini "lasagna	**Curried Kale**	**Peach Cobbler**
6	**Blueberry lavender lemonade**	Fruit Salad Slaw	Red Lentil Dahl	**Quick Pesto**	**Roasted Cinnamon Pineapple**
7	**Pancakes**	Chicken Salad	Maple syrup sage carrots	**Rosemary-Sage Crackers**	**Healthy Cinnamon Carrot Cookies**

15.3 Week 3

Day	Breakfast	Lunch	Dinner	Snacks	Dessert
1	Pancakes	Rosemary Chicken	Tasty Baked Fish	Sweet Potato Fries	Peach Cobbler
2	Eccentric Taste	Creamy Shrimp and Broccoli Fettuccine	Southwest Grain Bowl	Grilled Portobello Mushrooms	Roasted Cinnamon Pineapple
3	Blueberry Blast Smoothie	Tofu Fingers	Shrimp Fried Rice	Fruit Salsa	Healthy Cinnamon Carrot Cookies
4	Omelettes	Shrimp and Apple Stir Fry	Chicken Tikka	Easy Blueberry-Lemon Parfait	Easy Pumpkin Cheesecake
5	Blueberry Muffins	Lemon Oregano Chicke	Grilled Salmon with Herb Crust	Easy Blueberry-Lemon Parfait	Apple Cake
6	Easy Apple Oatmeal	Roasted Spaghetti Squash With Kale	Chicken Chili Stew	Creamy Strawberry Snacks	Pumpkin Cheesecake Bars
7	Deviled eggs	Zucchini Pancake	Chicken and Rice Casserole	Dill Carrots	Apple Crisp

15.4 Week 4

Day	Breakfast	Lunch	Dinner	Snacks	Dessert
1	Dilly Scrambled Eggs	Mushroom Soup	Quick and Easy Chicken Stir-Fry	Easy Blueberry-Lemon Parfait	Strawberry Pudding
2	Easy Apple Oatmeal	Simple Cabbage Soup	Parmesan roasted cauliflower	Creamy Strawberry Snacks	Arroz Con Leche
3	Pancakes	Garden Salad	Yogurt Covered Fruit Salad	Dill Carrots	Cherry Coffee Cake
4	Blueberry lavender lemonade	Chicken Wild Rice Asparagus Soup	Linguine with Garlic and Shrimp	Almond Pecan Caramel Popcorn	Muffins
5	Omelettes	Summer zucchini "lasagna	Eggplant and Tofu Stir-Fry	Sweet Potato Fries	Sweet Custard
6	Tofu and Kale scramble	Red Lentil Dahl	Fruit Salad Slaw	Grilled Portobello Mushrooms	Blueberry Whipped Pie
7	Loaded Veggie Eggs	Maple syrup sage carrots	Chicken Salad	Fruit Salsa	Fudge

15.5 Week 5

Day	Breakfast	Lunch	Dinner	Snacks	Dessert
1	Blueberry Muffins	Tasty Baked Fish	Rosemary Chicken	Sweet Potato Fries	Easy Pumpkin Cheesecake
2	Porridge	Southwest Grain Bowl	Creamy Shrimp and Broccoli Fettuccine	Grilled Portobello Mushrooms	Apple Cake
3	Energy Bars	Shrimp Fried Rice	Tofu Fingers	Fruit Salsa	Pumpkin Cheesecake Bars
4	Strawberry mockarita	Chicken Tikka	Shrimp and Apple Stir Fry	Easy Blueberry-Lemon Parfait	Apple Crisp
5	Egg White French Toast	Grilled Salmon with Herb Crust	Lemon Oregano Chicke	Easy Blueberry-Lemon Parfait	Peach Cobbler
6	Easy Apple Oatmeal	Chicken Chili Stew	Roasted Spaghetti Squash With Kale	Creamy Strawberry Snacks	Roasted Cinnamon Pineapple
7	Deviled eggs	Chicken and Rice Casserole	Zucchini Pancake	Dill Carrots	Healthy Cinnamon Carrot Cookies

15.6 Week 6

Day	Breakfast	Lunch	Dinner	Snacks	Dessert
1	Energy Bars	Mushroom Soup	Rosemary Chicken	Easy Blueberry-Lemon Parfait	Muffins
2	Blueberry Blast Smoothie	Simple Cabbage Soup	Creamy Shrimp and Broccoli Fettuccine	Creamy Strawberry Snacks	Sweet Custard
3	Loaded Veggie Eggs		Tofu Fingers	Dill Carrots	Blueberry Whipped Pie
4	Egg White French Toast	Chicken Wild Rice Asparagus Soup	Shrimp and Apple Stir Fry	Almond Pecan Caramel Popcorn	Fudge
5	Dilly Scrambled Eggs	Summer zucchini "lasagna	Lemon Oregano Chicke	Sweet Potato Fries	Apple Crisp
6	Blueberry lavender lemonade	Red Lentil Dahl	Roasted Spaghetti Squash With Kale	Grilled Portobello Mushrooms	Peach Cobbler
7	Omelettes	Maple syrup sage carrots	Zucchini Pancake	Fruit Salsa	Roasted Cinnamon Pineapple

15.7 Week 7

Day	Breakfast	Lunch	Dinner	Snacks	Dessert
1	Blueberry Muffins	Rosemary Chicken	Quick and Easy Chicken Stir-Fry	Sweet Potato Fries	Strawberry Pudding
2	Porridge	Creamy Shrimp and Broccoli Fettuccine	Parmesan roasted cauliflower	Grilled Portobello Mushrooms	Arroz Con Leche
3	Energy Bars	Tofu Fingers		Fruit Salsa	Cherry Coffee Cake
4	Strawberry mockarita	Shrimp and Apple Stir Fry	Linguine with Garlic and Shrimp	Easy Blueberry-Lemon Parfait	Muffins
5	Egg White French Toast	Lemon Oregano Chicke	Eggplant and Tofu Stir-Fry	Creamy Strawberry Snacks	Easy Pumpkin Cheesecake
6	Easy Apple Oatmeal	Roasted Spaghetti Squash With Kale	Fruit Salad Slaw	Dill Carrots	Apple Cake
7	Deviled eggs	Zucchini Pancake	Chicken Salad	Almond Pecan Caramel Popcorn	Pumpkin Cheesecake Bars

15.8 Week 8

Day	Breakfast	Lunch	Dinner	Snacks	Dessert
1	Deviled eggs	Rosemary Chicken	Mushroom Soup	Spiced Almonds and Cashews	Arroz Con Leche
2	Dilly Scrambled Eggs	Creamy Shrimp and Broccoli Fettuccine	Simple Cabbage Soup	Sweet Potato Fries	Cherry Coffee Cake
3	Loaded Veggie Eggs	Tofu Fingers		Spicy Crunch and Munch Snack Mix	Muffins
4	Easy Apple Oatmeal	Shrimp and Apple Stir Fry	Chicken Wild Rice Asparagus Soup	Sweet and Spicy Tortilla Chips	Easy Pumpkin Cheesecake
5	Egg White French Toast	Lemon Oregano Chicke	Summer zucchini "lasagna	Curried Kale	Apple Cake
6	Omelettes	Roasted Spaghetti Squash With Kale	Red Lentil Dahl	Quick Pesto	Pumpkin Cheesecake Bars
7	Blueberry Muffins	Zucchini Pancake	Maple syrup sage carrots	Rosemary-Sage Crackers	Roasted Cinnamon Pineapple

15.9 Week 9

Day	Breakfast	Lunch	Dinner	Snacks	Dessert
1	Blueberry Muffins	Mushroom Soup	Rosemary Chicken	Blasted Brussels Sprouts	Cherry Coffee Cake
2	Porridge	Simple Cabbage Soup	Creamy Shrimp and Broccoli Fettuccine	Dilled Cream Cheese Spread	Muffins
3	Energy Bars		Tofu Fingers	Easy Blueberry-Lemon Parfait	Easy Pumpkin Cheesecake
4	Strawberry mockarita	Chicken Wild Rice Asparagus Soup	Shrimp and Apple Stir Fry	Edamole Spread	Apple Cake
5	Egg White French Toast	Summer zucchini "lasagna	Lemon Oregano Chicke	Fruit Salsa	Apple Crisp
6	Easy Apple Oatmeal	Red Lentil Dahl	Roasted Spaghetti Squash With Kale	Green Beans with Hazelnuts and Dried Cranberries	Peach Cobbler
7	Deviled eggs	Maple syrup sage carrots	Zucchini Pancake	Grilled Portobello Mushrooms	Roasted Cinnamon Pineapple

15.10 Week 10

Day	Breakfast	Lunch	Dinner	Snacks	Dessert
1	Energy Bars	Quick and Easy Chicken Stir-Fry	Rosemary Chicken	Roasted Pumpkin Seeds	Healthy Cinnamon Carrot Cookies
2	Blueberry Blast Smoothie	Parmesan roasted cauliflower	Creamy Shrimp and Broccoli Fettuccine	Almond Pecan Caramel Popcorn	Arroz Con Leche
3	Loaded Veggie Eggs		Tofu Fingers	BBQ Winter Squash	Cherry Coffee Cake
4	Egg White French Toast	Linguine with Garlic and Shrimp	Shrimp and Apple Stir Fry	Black-Eyed Peas	Muffins
5	Dilly Scrambled Eggs	Eggplant and Tofu Stir-Fry	Lemon Oregano Chicke	Dill Carrots	Easy Pumpkin Cheesecake
6	Blueberry lavender lemonade	Fruit Salad Slaw	Roasted Spaghetti Squash With Kale	Curried Kale	Apple Cake
7	Omelettes	Chicken Salad	Zucchini Pancake	Creamy Strawberry Snacks	Pumpkin Cheesecake Bars

16MEASUREMENT CONVERSION CHART

Weight

Metric	Imperial
15 g	½ oz.
30 g	1 oz.
60g	2 oz.
90 g	3 oz.
125g	4oz.
175g	6 oz.
250g	8 oz.
300g	10 oz.
375 g	12 oz.
400 g	13 oz.
425 g	14 oz.
500 g	1 lb
750 g	1½ lb
1 kg	2lb

Liquid Measures

Quantity	Metric
1 teaspoon	5ml
1 tablespoon	15 ml
¼ cup	60 ml
1/3 cup	80 ml
½ cup	125 ml
1 cup	250 ml
1-¼ cup	300 ml
1½ cup	375 ml
1-2/3 cup	400 ml
1¾ cup	450 ml
2 cups	500 ml
2½ cups	600 ml
3 cups	750 ml

17CONCLUSION

Both abrupt and persistent damage might result in kidney failure. Numerous factors, including diabetes, high blood pressure, using a lot of medications, being severely dehydrated, renal injury, and other disorders, can lead to kidney failure. Kidney disease progresses via five stages. From severe renal failure to relatively modest situations, these could exist. As the stages progress, the symptoms and problems get worse. If you have renal failure, you can talk to your doctor about the best course of treatment for your condition.

BONUS: Scanning the following QR code will take you to a web page where you can access 8 fantastic bonuses after leaving your email and an honest review of my book on Amazon: 4 online courses about renal diet and recipes and 4 mobile apps about renal diet.

Link: https://dl.bookfunnel.com/91d0m4nnrw

Printed in Great Britain
by Amazon

Printed in Great Britain
by Amazon

18333885R00052